THE TIME AND PLACE OF BAPTISM

A HISTORICAL SYNOPSIS AND A COMMENTARY

THE CATHOLIC UNIVERSITY OF AMERICA

CANON LAW STUDIES

No. 324

The Time and Place of Baptism

A Historical Synopsis and a Commentary

BY

REV. WALTER J. CONWAY, A.B., J.C.L.
PRIEST OF THE ARCHDIOCESE OF PHILADELPHIA

A DISSERTATION

SUBMITTED TO THE FACULTY OF THE SCHOOL OF CANON LAW OF THE CATHOLIC UNIVERSITY OF AMERICA IN PARTIAL FULFILLMENT OF THE REQUIREMENTS FOR THE DEGREE OF DOCTOR OF CANON LAW

THE CATHOLIC UNIVERSITY OF AMERICA PRESS
WASHINGTON, D. C.
1954

NIHIL OBSTAT:

CLEMENS V. BASTNAGEL, S.T.L., J.U.D.
Censor Deputatus

Washingtonii, D. C., die 18 Mart. 1953

IMPRIMATUR:

✠ JOHN FRANCIS O'HARA, C.S.C.
Archiepiscopus Philadelphiensis
Philadelphiae, 19 Mart. 1953

Copyright 1954
THE CATHOLIC UNIVERSITY OF AMERICA PRESS, INC.

MURRAY AND HEISTER
WASHINGTON, D. C.

PRINTED BY
TIMES AND NEWS PUBLISHING CO.
GETTYSBURG, PA., U.S.A.

TABLE OF CONTENTS

TABLE OF CONTENTS (Continued)

CANONICAL COMMENTARY

TABLE OF CONTENTS (Continued)

FOREWORD

When Jesus Christ founded His Church, He entrusted to it the dispensation of His sacraments, which He had instituted as a means for obtaining the divine grace that is so essential to the attainment and development of the supernatural life. Throughout the centuries the Church has been constantly solicitous for the supernatural life of man, and thus it has exercised great prudence and care in the administration of the sacraments.

Since baptism is the foundation of all the other sacraments, and the gateway through which the supernatural life is first acquired, and through which the graces of all the other sacraments flow, the Church, in its legislation, has adequately provided for the valid and licit administration of this sacrament. In regard to some of the requirements for the licit administration of baptism, the Church, in its desire to enhance the sacrament with solemnity, reverence and propriety, has, from early times, laid down certain norms for the time and place of baptism.

It is the purpose of this dissertation to present the legislation of the Church concerning the proper time and place of baptism from Apostolic times to the present day. In the treatment of the element of time, not only the legislation of the Church concerning the proper days for the administration of baptism will be considered, but also, in regard to infants, the period of time between their birth and the reception of this sacrament, and, in regard to adults, the period of time spent in preparation for baptism. In addition to the prescriptions of time and place concerning the solemn administration of baptism, the judicious provisions in the law of the Church for extraordinary cases will be considered.

The writer takes this occasion to express his appreciation for the opportunity to pursue graduate studies in the School of Canon Law at The Catholic University of America. He particularly expresses his sincere gratitude to the members of the Faculty of the School of Canon Law for the encouragement and assistance which they rendered in the preparation of this work, and to all others who in any way contributed by interest and aid towards the completion of this dissertation.

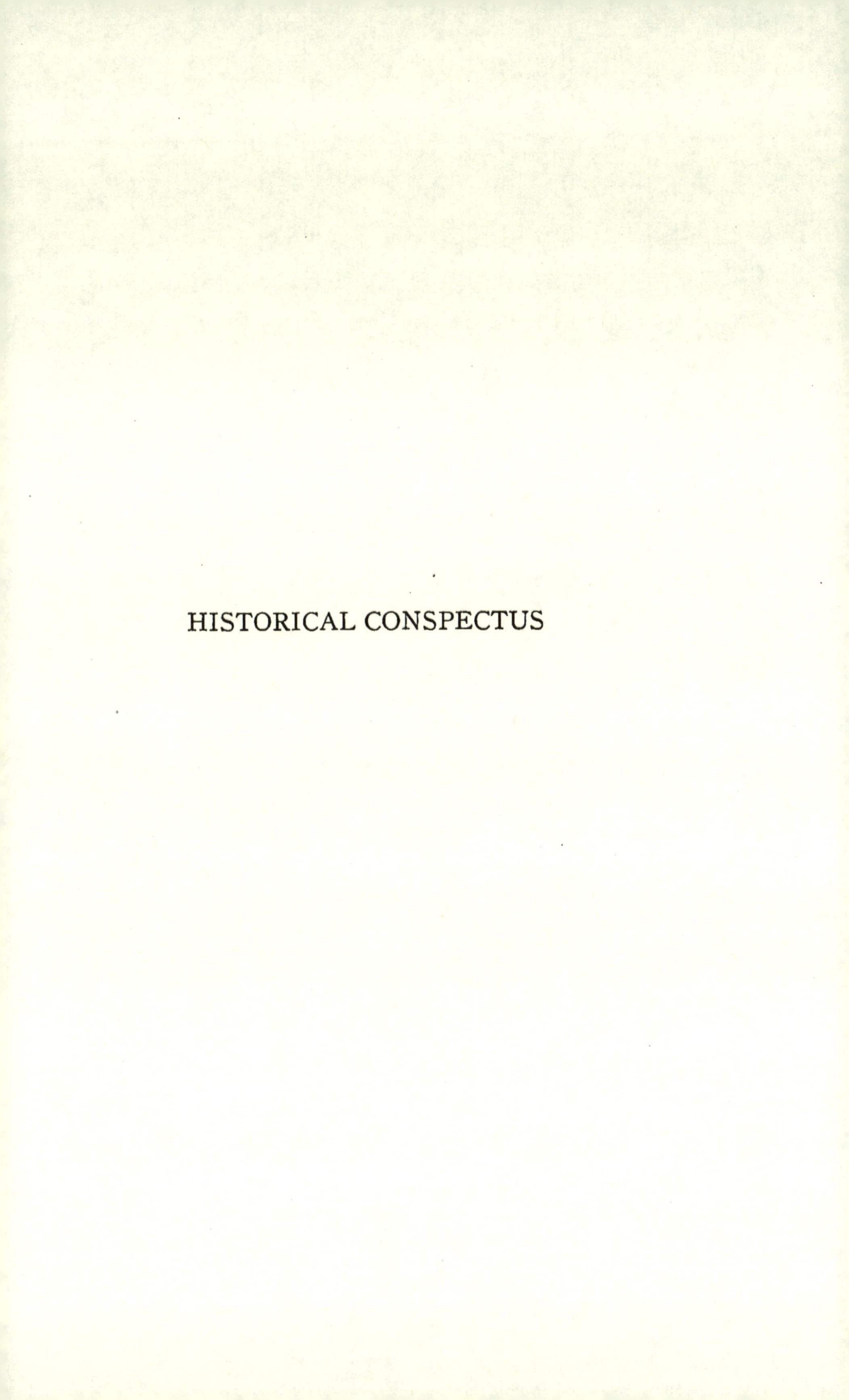

HISTORICAL CONSPECTUS

CHAPTER I

The Time of Baptism From the Apostolic Age to the Council of Trent

SECT. I. THE TIME OF BAPTISM IN THE APOSTOLIC AGE

When Christ gave the twofold command to His Apostles to teach all nations and to baptize them,[1] He did not in any way determine the particular circumstances of time in which they should confer this sacrament by which all men are made members of His Church. As a consequence, there is not to be found any indication in Sacred Scripture, neither in the Acts of the Apostles, nor in the Epistles of St. Paul, of the observance of any particular hour, day or period of the year as the proper time for the administration of baptism. Nor did the Apostles assign any special occasion for baptism, but they themselves baptized when the opportunity presented itself, or when occasion required it. A comparison of the history of the Acts of the Apostles and the subsequent history of the Church indicates that the Apostles left this circumstance of time wholly to the judgment and prudence of their successors in the Church.[2] Corblet (1819-1886) supported this same view in saying that he did not believe there was any determined period of time for baptism in the first two centuries.[3]

When St. Peter spoke to the multitude of people of all nations on that first Christian Pentecost and instructed them in the doctrine of the Divinity of Jesus Christ, he did not wait for any special time to baptize them. Rather, when they asked Peter and the other Apostles what they should do, Peter took the oppor-

---

[1] Matt., XXVIII:19.

[2] Bingham, *The Antiquities of the Christian Church* (edited by the Rev. Robert Bingham, 10 vols., Oxford, 1885), III, 112.

[3] *Histoire dogmatique, liturgique, et archéologique du sacrement de baptême* (2 vols., Paris, 1881-1882), I, 476 (hereafter cited as *Histoire du sacrement de baptême*).

tunity to tell them to repent and to be baptized. The *Acts of the Apostles* show that three thousand persons were instructed and baptized on the same day.[4]

After Philip had instructed the eunuch in the glad tidings of Jesus, concerning Whom the prophet Isaias had spoken in Scripture, he immediately baptized the eunuch in the water by the wayside.[5] Ananias, having been instructed in a vision to baptize St. Paul, waited for no particular occasion or time to perform the baptism. Rather, Sacred Scripture indicates that he immediately departed, entered into the house of Paul, and baptized him.[6]

From the Acts of the Apostles there is sufficient proof to show that there were no special times for the administration of baptism, but that these were determined by the varying circumstances which occurred during the early days of the establishment of Christianity. St. Ambrose (+397) noted this difference between the first and later centuries in the discipline of the Church in respect to the time of baptism. As occasion required it, he observed, baptism was conferred on any day or at any time.[7]

In dissuading men from the indefinite deferring of baptism, under the pretext of observing the fixed times appointed by the Church for its more solemn administration, this greater liberty of the Apostolic times is often pointed to as furnishing proof to the contrary.[8]

SECT. II. THE DAYS FOR THE ADMINISTRATION OF BAPTISM

Art. 1. Easter and Pentecost the Traditional Times of Baptism

Corblet thought that the feasts of Easter and of Pentecost were preferred for reasons of liturgical convenience, and that what

[4] Acts of the Apostles, II:1-41.

[5] Acts, VIII:38.

[6] Acts, IX:18.

[7] *Commentarium in Eph.,* IV (v. 11, 12)—J. P. Migne, *Patrologiae Cursus Completus, Series Latina* (221 vols., Parisiis, 1844-1864), XVII, 388 (hereafter referred to as *MPL*).

[8] St. Basil, *Homilia XIII, Exhortatoria ad sanctum baptisma*—J. P. Migne, *Patrologiae Cursus Completus, Series Graeca* (161 vols., Parisiis, 1857-1866), XXXI, 425 (hereafter referred to as *MPG*).

in the beginning had connoted only a facultative use became at a later time more and more a matter of ecclesiastical law.[9] But what seems to have been the cause for the setting of determined times relative to the conferring of baptism was the fact that later converts lacked the zeal and readiness of the first converts. After the first century the Church found it necessary to act more slowly in the preparation of candidates for baptism. Because of the dullness of these candidates the Church had to give longer and more detailed instructions, and also because of their frequent relapse the Church had to make the period of probation somewhat longer for them.[10] As a consequence, the Church established special days on which the great number of candidates, after such long and exacting preparations, could be baptized together. St. Ambrose also observed the fact that even though there was no special season of the year for the administration of baptism during Apostolic times, yet, when the Church spread into many parts of the world and oratories were built, baptism was administered only on determined days, except for those who were sick.[11]

Tertullian (ca. 155-ca. 235) was the first among the Christian writers to make any mention of a particular period of time as being set aside for the solemn administration of baptism.[12] In speaking on this point, Tertullian stated that the Pasch offers the more regular occasion for baptism, since the Passion of Our Lord, in which we are baptized, was consummated at that time. And Pentecost offers the other occasion, since by then the Lord's Resurrection was widely made known, and the gift of the Holy Spirit was received.[13]

He indicated these two dates without invoking any tradition in his favor; rather, he assigned for these dates a dogmatic rea-

---

[9] *Histoire du sacrement de baptême,* I, 476.

[10] Bingham, *The Antiquities of the Christian Church,* IV, 113.

[11] *Commentarium in Ephes.,* IV (V. 11, 12)—*MPL,* XVII, 388.

[12] W. Smith and S. Cheetham, *Dictionary of Christian Antiquities* (2 vols., Toronto, 1880), I, 165.

[13] *De baptismo,* XIX—*Corpus Scriptorum Ecclesiasticorum Latinorum* (Vindabonae, 1866—; Vol. XX, edd. A. Reifferscheid, G. Wissowa, 1890), XX, 217 (hereafter cited *CV* [*Corpus Vindoboninse*]); *MPL,* I, 1222.

son.[14] This indeed indicates that by the time of Tertullian Easter and Pentecost were well established and determined by custom as the proper days for the administration of baptism. In conjunction with his statement concerning Easter and Pentecost as the proper time for baptism, Tertullian also clearly indicated that the conferring of baptism was not restricted to any set hour or day, but that any season was suitable for baptism.[15]

The Fathers of the Church made repeated references to the periods of Easter and Pentecost as being the special times for the solemn administration of baptism. St. Jerome (ca. 342-420) in commenting on the prophecy of Zachary concerning the "living water" that would go out of Jerusalem in summer and winter, applied this to the two solemn times of baptism, Easter and Pentecost, the former of which is in the spring and the other in the summer.[16] St. Augustine (354-430), among the western Fathers, and St. Basil (330-379), and St. Cyril of Jerusalem (313-386), among the eastern Fathers, also spoke of these two feasts as special days for solemnly conferring baptism.[17]

It is claimed by some authors that the time for baptism during the early ages was not confined to the actual day of Easter or Pentecost, but that the whole period of fifty days between Easter and Pentecost was considered as but one solemn season for baptism.[18] In substantiation of their opinion they pointed to the words of Tertullian.[19] Corblet claimed that many of the councils of the

---

[14] Bareille, "Baptême d'apres les Pères Grecs et Latins," *Dictionnaire de théologie catholique* (15 vols., incomplete, Paris: Letouzey et Ané, 1903—), II, 212 (hereafter cited *DTC*).

[15] *De baptismo,* XIX: "Caeterum omnis dies domini est, omnis hora, omne tempus habile baptismo, si de solemnitate interest, de gratia nihil refert."—*CV,* XX, 217; *MPL,* I, 1222.

[16] *Commentarium in Zachariam,* Lib. III, cap. XIV—*MPL,* XXV, 1528; Bingham, *The Antiquities of the Christian Church,* IV, 106.

[17] St. Augustinus, *In Quadragesima,* VI, *MPL,* XXXVIII, 1048; St. Basilius, *De Baptismo,* XIII, 1 Hom.—*MPG,* XXXI, 424; St. Cyrillus, *Catechesis XVIII,* 32—*MPG,* XXXIII, 1053.

[18] Bingham, *op. cit.,* IV, 108; Corblet, *Histoire du sacrement de baptême,* I, 478.

[19] *De baptismo,* XIX: "Exinde Pentecoste ordinandis lavacris latissimum spatium est, quo et Domini resurrectio inter discipulos frequentata est, et gratia Spiritus Sancti dedicata."—*CV,* XX, 217, *MPL,* I, 1222.

Church precisely named Easter and Pentecost as the days for conferring baptism. But he also maintained that these councils for the most part used very general terms and expressions for these two days, so that they seemed to refer to a whole season rather than to any particular day.[20]

In the third century there is further evidence for the theory that the time for baptism attached to other days besides Easter. During this period, in Africa, the Easter feast lasted for eight days, and it was during this period of time that baptism was conferred.[21]

Corblet believed that, if indeed in the beginning solemn baptism was conferred only at Easter and Pentecost, then in the course of the years, when the number of candidates became very great, the baptism of some of them must have been remitted to the days during the week following these feasts. He observed that in Syria the baptism of adults was remitted to the Monday after Easter, or the Monday after Pentecost.[22]

From a comparison of the customs of the various churches in the western world, the fact is easily recognized that Roman usage was always more strict in its adherence to Easter and Pentecost as the established days of baptism than the usage of any of the other churches. The church of Rome always urged the restrictive practice and made repeated efforts through the popes, the bishops and the councils to confine the solemn administration of baptism to Easter and Pentecost.

At just what time the vigils of Easter and of Pentecost supplanted the actual feasts of Easter and Pentecost as the proper days for baptism is not known. Gratian, however, in his comment on the letter of Pope Siricius (385-398) to Himerius, Bishop of Tarragona, understood the Pope to specify the vigils of these

---

[20] Corblet, *op. cit.*, I, 479.

[21] St. Victorius Papa (189-198), *Epist. ad Theophilum Alexandriae*: "A quartadecima vero luna primi mensis, usque ad vicessimum primum eiusdem mensis diem, eadem celebretur festivitas. Eodem vero tempore baptismus celebrandus est Catholicus."—Mansi, *Sacrorum Conciliorum nova et amplissima collectio* (53 vols. in 59, Parisiis, Arvhemii, Lipsiae, 1901-1927), I, 701 (hereafter referred to as Mansi).

[22] *Histoire du sacrement de baptême*, I, 479.

feasts.[23] It simply stated, with reference to any and all of the churches, that baptism was to be conferred at Easter and Pentecost.[24] Leo the Great (440-461), when writing to the bishops of Sicily, stated that the two seasons of Easter and Pentecost are the seasons legitimately established by the Roman Pontiff for the conferring of baptism. He warned the bishops that they should not add any other days to this particular observance of the solemn administration of baptism.[25] Again, Pope Gelasius (492-496), in a letter to the bishops of Lucania, stated that it was not allowed to anyone at any time to confer the venerable sacrament of baptism except at the Paschal and Pentecostal festivals, unless there emerged a case of dangerous sickness, from which death would probably ensue.[26]

Moreover, Pope Gregory II (715-731), who lived later than two centuries after the above mentioned Popes, still spoke of the feasts of Easter and Pentecost as the only days on which the sacrament of baptism could be administered outside of a case of urgent danger of death.[27] A century later, Pope Nicholas I (858-867) still mentioned the continued existence of the two traditional times of the year in which baptism was administered, namely Easter and Pentecost. In this letter Pope Nicholas made specific mention of Holy Saturday and of the Eve of Pentecost as the actual days for the administration of baptism.[28]

These repeated papal regulations indicate the strong tenacity with which the Roman Church adhered to the traditional seasons

---

[23] C. 11, D. IV, *de cons.*

[24] Jaffé, *Regesta Pontificum Romanorum ab condita ecclesia ad annum post Christum natum MCXCVIII* (2. ed. by F. Kaltenbrunner [to the year 590], P. Ewald [590-882], and S. Loewenfeld [882-1198] and so referred to as JK, JE, and JL, 2 vols. in 1, Lipsiae, 1885-1888), JK, n. 255; *MPL,* XIII, 1131; Mansi, III, 655.

[25] *Epistola IV,* c. 5—JK, n. 414; Mansi, V, 1305, *MPL,* LIV, 695; c. XII, D. IV, *de cons.*

[26] JK, n. 636; *MPL,* LVI, 691; c. XVIII, D. IV, *de cons.*

[27] *Ad clerum, ordinem, et plebem Thuringiae*—Mansi, XII, 240; *Monumenta Germaniae Historica* (*MGH*) (*Hanoverae,* 1826—), *Epistolae* (*Ep.*) (7 vols., 1887-1928), III (ed. E. Dümmler, 1899), 267; JE, n. 2161.

[28] *Reponsa ad Bulgaros,* c. 69—JE, n. 2812; Mansi, XV, 425; *MGH,* Ep., VI (ed. E. Perels, 1925), 591.

of Easter and Pentecost as the proper times for baptism. The practice continued for several more centuries, and in England this tradition was given its continued support as late as the thirteenth century. In consequence of an existing superstitious belief, some taught that it was dangerous to confer baptism, especially on children, during those two seasons. This superstition Cardinal Otho, the papal delegate, firmly denounced in the Council of London (1237) as contrary to the practice of the Pope, who himself solemnly baptized at these times, and also as contrary to the practices of the Church in other parts of the world.[29]

In order to enforce the liturgical laws which had existed since the second century for the determining of the seasons of the year for the administering of baptism, a series of provincial councils, convened in different parts of the West from the sixth to the thirteenth centuries, included canons and decrees concerning this factor in their legislation. The first council to make such legislation was the Council of Gerona, in Spain, which was held in the year 517. In this council it was decreed that catechumens were to be baptized on the feasts of Easter and Pentecost, and that only the sick were to be baptized on other solemn feasts.[30]

Later in the century the Synod of Auxerre (ca. 580), in Gaul, used strong language to enforce this liturgical law. One of its decrees forbade that anyone who was not in danger of death should receive baptism at any season of the year other than the Easter season. Persons who insisted in a contumacious manner on bringing their children to the churches for baptism were not to receive absolution in the sacrament of penance. Furthermore, the Synod stated that any priest who presumed to receive such people in their request for their children's baptism if they lacked the permission of the proper ecclesiastical authorities should be excommunicated for three months.[31] Similar legislation was enacted in

---

[29] Canon III—Mansi, XXIII, 449.

[30] Canon 4—Bruns, *Canones Apostolorum et Conciliorum Saeculorum IV-VII* (2 vols., Berolini, 1839), II, 19 (hereafter cited as Bruns); c. XV, D. IV, *de cons.*

[31] Canon 18—Bruns, II, 239; Mansi, IX, 913.

the II Council of Mâcon (585), in Gaul, which demanded that baptism should be conferred only during the Easter season.[32]

Over two centuries later the Councils of Mainz, the first in the year 813,[33] the second in the year 847,[34] both cited in canons of their legislation the decrees of Pope Leo the Great, who had determined the two seasons of the year, Easter and Pentecost, as the proper time for the administering of baptism.

The provincial council which was held in Paris in the year 829 also made similar legislation concerning the two seasons for baptism.[35] Similar legislation was made by the Council of Worms (868)[36] and the Council of Tribur (895).[37] Only one exception did they allow to this law, namely baptism conferred to one in danger of death. In 1072 the Council of Rouen, in France, regulated the early decrees of Pope Innocent I (401-417)[38] and Pope Leo the Great by ordering that adults indeed were to be baptized on the festivals of Easter and Pentecost, but that infants were to be baptized at whatever day the parents sought baptism for them.[39]

In England the Council of Chelsea (Cealchythe, 787),[40] the Council of Winchester (1074)[41] and the Council of London (1237)[42] all affirmed the legislation of the previous councils held in western Europe, by legislating that baptism was to be administered only in the seasons of Easter and Pentecost.

All the councils here mentioned, except two, maintained that baptism was to be administered only at Easter and Pentecost. The Synod of Auxerre (ca. 580) and the II Council of Mâcon

---

[32] Canon 3—Mansi, IX, 951.
[33] Canon 4—Mansi, XIV, 16.
[34] Canon 1—Mansi, XIV, 903.
[35] Cap. I, Canon 7—Mansi, XIV, 541.
[36] Canon 1—Mansi, XV, 869.
[37] Canon 12—Mansi, XVIII, 138.
[38] *Epistola ad Victricium Rotomagensem Episcopum,* c. IX—*MPL,* XX, 476.
[39] Canon 24—Mansi, XX, 40.
[40] Canon 2—Mansi, XII, 939.
[41] Canon 7—Mansi, XX, 440.
[42] Canon 3—Mansi, XXIII, 449.

(585) are to be excepted from this group, since they pointed explicitly to the practice of baptizing only during the Easter season. In fact, they interdicted priests who presumed, outside of a case of necessity, to baptize during any time other than the season of Easter. As an explanation for this exception there may be offered the opinion of Corblet (1819-1886), namely that the administration of baptism during the season of Pentecost fell into desuetude in these particular dioceses.[43] But Bingham (1668-1723) seemed to offer a more harmonious explanation by stating that in these councils the term "Easter time" is to be understood to include also the fifty days after Easter up to and including the feast of Pentecost.[44] Suarez (1548-1617), too, had claimed that, even though there was no mention of Pentecost, this silence did not necessarily exclude consideration of it.[45] He cited Rupertus (1070-1129), Abbot of the Monastery of Deutz (1120-1129), in support of his claim. This abbot absolutely stated that there was a custom in the Church of baptizing only at Easter,[46] but later on in another place added that the custom of baptizing was observed also at Pentecost.[47]

In conjunction with papal and conciliar legislation, there was also from time to time some special imperial or episcopal legislation concerning the liturgical days for administering baptism. Foremost among the canons of the imperial legislation is a canon in the Capitularies of Charlemagne, given at Salz (in Thuringia) in 804. This canon prescribed that, except in a case of sickness, no one was to be given baptism outside of the Easter and Pentecostal seasons.[48] The collection of Capitularies of Benedict the Levite prescribed in one section that baptism was to be conferred only in the two seasons, Easter and Pentecost, as established by

---

[43] *Histoire du sacrement de baptême,* I, 480.

[44] *The Antiquities of the Christian Church,* IV, 108.

[45] *Commentarii et Disputationes,* Quest. LXXI, Disp. XXX, sect. II—*Opera Omnia* (26 vols. in 28, editio nova a Carolo Berton, Paris: L. Vivès, 1856-1868), XX, 576.

[46] *De Divinis Officiis,* Lib. 4, cap. 18—*MPL,* CLXX, 112.

[47] *Op. cit.,* Lib. 10, cap. 2—MPL, CLXX, 263.

[48] *Capitula Data Presbyteris,* canon 10—*MPL,* XCVII, 276.

the Sovereign Pontiff.[49] In another section of this collection, it was stated that no one was to presume to confer baptism except on the Vigils of Easter and Pentecost.[50]

Sometimes bishops made this observance a matter of special injunction to the clergy at their ordination. In the seventh century St. Ildefonsus, Archbishop of Toledo (657-667), warned his clergy that they should baptize only in the seasons of Easter and Pentecost; outside of these two seasons, baptism could be conferred only in consequence of the necessity occasioned through a dangerous illness.[51] Hérard, Archbishop of Tours (855-870), prescribed in his Capitularies, in the year 858, that the clergy of his diocese should baptize only at Easter and Pentecost.[52]

During the early ages of the Church, especially from the second to the fifth century, it was very advantageous for the Church to have two special periods designated for the administration of baptism. During these times a multitude of adults were converted to Christianity, and these needed special and long periods of instruction and probation. As a consequence, the Church arranged these preparatory periods so that they would terminate at the commencement of one or the other of these special seasons for baptism. As was to be expected, the number to be baptized was greater at Easter than at Pentecost, for the period between Pentecost and Easter was much longer than those fifty days between Easter and Pentecost.

Nevertheless, in the course of the progress of the centuries and the spread and development of the Church, the baptism of adults became rare and exceptional. The baptism of infants in these later centuries became more and more common, and such had to be baptized rather early after birth because of the greater danger of death during the period following birth. Accordingly, the limitation and restriction of the conferring of baptism to the seasons of Easter and Pentecost, as imposed by liturgical law, came to have less significance, and gradually, both in the Church

---

[49] Lib. I, 171—*MPL,* XCVII, 722.

[50] Lib. II, 181—*MPL,* XCVII, 769.

[51] *De Cognitione Baptismi,* Lib. I, Cap. 108—*MPL,* XCVI, 157.

[52] Martène, *De Antiquis Ecclesiae Ritibus* (4 vols., Rotomagi, 1700), I, 2.

of the East and of the West, these seasons ceased to be the only absolute times, outside of necessity, during which baptism was to be conferred.

Suarez claimed that this custom lasted up to the time of Charlemagne (+814), and then began to be abolished as altogether antiquated.[53] Martène (1654-1739) stated that this custom continued until the end of the eleventh century, at which time it became abrogated.[54] He cited the testimony of Theophilactus, an eleventh century writer, in support of his statement.[55] From the testimony of Rupertus, Abbot of Deutz (1120-1129), one can easily understand the reason on account of which this custom was changed. He stated that the great danger of dying without the sacrament, especially in the case of infants, alarmed so many that the Church could no longer command them to wait until a special season.[56]

Nicephorus Callistus Xanthopulus (ca. 1256-ca. 1335) stated that even at that time the custom of conferring baptism only during the Easter season was observed solely in Thessaly. He added that on account of this continuing custom many died before they had received the sacrament.[57] Likewise, despite all opinions to the contrary, in England in the thirteenth century it was still required that solemn baptism be conferred at Easter and Pentecost, as long as a case of necessity did not intervene.[58] For the most part, however, with some exceptions, this custom as a precept had ceased by the eleventh century. Nevertheless, the custom of solemnly baptizing at Easter and Pentecost still continued in the later centuries to be observed in some places out of deference to the ancient laws of the Church, provided there was not any danger of death, and the catechumen happened to have just completed his preparation for baptism at the commencement of the festivities of Easter or of Pentecost.

---

[53] *Commentarii et Disputationes,* Quest. LXXI, Disp. XXX, Sect. II—*Opera Omnia,* XX, 577.

[54] *De Antiquis Ecclesiae Ritibus,* I, 6.

[55] *Commentarium in Lucam,* canon 10—*MPG,* CXXIII, 834.

[56] *De Divinis Officiis,* Lib. 4, cap. 18—*MPL,* CLXX, 112.

[57] *Historia Ecclesiastica,* Lib. XII, cap. 34—*MPG,* CXLVI, 862.

[58] Council of London (1237), canon 3—Mansi, XXIII, 449.

Art. 2. The Extension of the Proper Time of Baptism to Other Days

There existed copious legislation, both of popes and of councils, that insisted upon the solemn administration of baptism at the proper seasons of Easter and Pentecost. In fact, for the most part the documents containing this legislation did not leave room for any exception outside of a case of necessity. Nevertheless, despite the firm statement of the canons and the decrees, there were numerous deviations from the law in different sections of the world in which the Church at that time was established. These deviations did not ignore or abolish the days proclaimed by the law as proper for the giving of baptism, but rather increased their number. Such an extension took place gradually and over the period of a few centuries.

In general, Easter and Pentecost were observed as the two special seasons for baptism in the Western Church. In the Eastern Church this same discipline was observed up until the fourth century, during which period it became customary to baptize also on the feast of the Epiphany.[59]

This custom was tolerated in the East by the Church of Rome. Later on, when, besides Easter and Pentecost, other seasons for the administration of baptism were introduced in the Western Church, these were really motivated by exceptional circumstances, and should accordingly be regarded more as a local custom, than as a general exception to the law of the early Church.[60]

The Greek Church was the first to add the feast of the Epiphany to the feasts of Easter and Pentecost as a special day for the administering of baptism. On this day there was commemorated in the Greek Church the baptism of Christ by St. John, and as a consequence this day was considered as a most fitting occasion for the administration of baptism to those who wished to become members of Christ's Church. St. John Chrysostom (344-407), Archbishop of Constantinople (398-407), clearly stated that the Epiphany was the day on which Christ received baptism and

---

[59] Martigny, *Dictionnaire des Antiquités Chrétiennes* (Paris, 1855), p. 68.
[60] Corblet, *Histoire du sacrement de baptême,* I, 481.

sanctified the waters.[61] Other Fathers also referred to the Epiphany in their enumeration of the celebrated times for baptism in the Greek Church.[62]

From the East the practice of conferring baptism on the feast of the Epiphany passed into Sicily, then into Africa, and finally into Spain.[63] Pope St. Leo the Great (440-461), in his letter to the bishops of Sicily, complained regarding the fact that as many were baptized on the feast of the Epiphany as at Easter. He termed such a custom an unreasonable novelty and a confusion of the mysteries of the two feasts of the Epiphany and Easter.[64] Victor, Bishop of Vita (in the African Province of Byzacena), who wrote in 485, plainly intimated that St. Eugene, Bishop of Carthage (480-505), baptized on the feast of the Epiphany. In his statement he did not expressly name the Epiphany, but he stated that the bishop conferred the sacrament on a feast before the Kalends of February, which was the fatal day on which African bishops were banished, and the churches destroyed by the Arians, in the time of the Vandalic persecution.[65] Corblet observed that this administration on the feast of the Epiphany was not motivated by the approach of persecution. Rather, he believed that it was a tolerated usage, since it lasted even up to the thirteenth century.[66]

Likewise the custom of baptizing on the feast of the Epiphany must have arisen in some parts of Spain, because Siricius (385-398) reported its observance as contrary to the laws of the Church, which commanded that baptism be conferred only on the feasts of Easter and Pentecost.[67] In Ireland in the fifth century

---

[61] *Homilia de Baptismo Christi*—*MPG,* XLIX, 365.

[62] St. Gregory of Nazianzen (329-389), *Oratio* XL—MPG, XXXVI, 370; St. John Chrysostom, *In Epist. ad Ephes.,* Cap. I, Hom. III—*MPG,* LXII, 25. St. Gregory of Nyssa (ca. 335-395), *In Baptismum Christi*—*MPG,* XIVI, 578.

[63] Bareille, "Baptême d'apres les Pères Grecs et Latins," *DTC,* II, 212.

[64] *Epistola* IV, c. I—JK, n. 414; Mansi, V, 1306; *MPL,* LIV, 695.

[65] *De Persecutione Vandalica,* Lib. II—*MPL,* LVIII, 201.

[66] *Histoire du sacrement de baptême,* I, 482.

[67] *Epistola ad Himerium,* I—JK, n. 255; *MPL,* XII, 1131; Mansi, III, 655; c. 11, D. IV, *de cons.*

there was the prevailing custom of baptizing on the feast of the Epiphany as well as at Easter and Pentecost.[68]

In France custom added to the feasts of Easter and Pentecost three other days on which baptism was solemnly administered, the feasts of the Epiphany, of Christmas and of the Nativity of St. John the Baptist.[69] St. Gregory of Tours (538-594) stated that the baptism of King Clovis (481-511) and the Franks took place on the feast of the Nativity of Our Lord.[70] Likewise St. Gregory furnished testimony that baptism was conferred on the feast of the Nativity of St. John the Baptist.[71] St. Augustine (+605), the Apostle of England, is reported to have baptized with the assistance of his missionaries more than ten thousand people on Christmas Day.[72] But this fact is considered rather an exceptional case in which a missionary was simply availing himself of an opportune time for baptizing the large number of people whom he converted. This opinion is further strengthened by the fact that all the Councils of England absolutely decreed Easter and Pentecost to be the only times in which baptism could be solemnly administered.[73]

Moreover, in some places in Spain the custom of baptizing on the feasts of the Apostles and Martyrs prevailed.[74] But this custom was condemned and forbidden particularly by Pope Siricius (384-398) when he wrote to Himerius,[75] and also by the Pope

---

[68] *Synodus alia Sancti Patricii (456)*, canon 19—Bruns, II, 307.

[69] Martène, *De antiquis Ecclesiae Ritibus,* I, 4.

[70] *Liber de Gloria Confessorum,* Cap. 69—*MPL,* LXXI, 878.

[71] *Historia Francorum,* Lib. 8, cap. 9: "Rogaverunt deinceps, ut ad sanctum Pascha baptizaretur, sed nec tunc allatus est infans. Deprecati sunt autem tertio, ut ad festivitatem Sancti Joannis exhiberetur, sed nec tunc venit."—*MPL,* LXXI, 453.

[72] Martène, *De Antiquis Ecclesiae Ritibus,* I, 4.

[73] Corblet, *Histoire du sacrement de baptême,* I, 482.

[74] Martène, *op. cit.,* I, 5.

[75] *Epistola ad Himerium,* I: "Non ratione auctoritatis aliciuius, sed sola temeritate presumitur, ut passim et libere . . . in Apostolorum seu martirum festivitatibus, innumerae plebes baptizentur"—JK, n. 255; Mansi, III, 655; c. 11, D. IV, *de cons.*

St. Leo the Great in his Epistle to the Bishops of Campania, Samnium and Picenum.[76]

Apparently this custom of baptizing on the feasts of the Apostles and Martyrs was observed also in Gaul in a few localities, for the II Council of Mâcon (585) expressly condemned the administration of baptism on those days.[77] In some churches there existed the custom of administering baptism also on the anniversary of the dedication of the church, in order to enhance the occasion with greater solemnity. This was the case at Jerusalem. Every year on the anniversary of the dedication of *The Church of the Resurrection,* built by Constantine over our Lord's grave, there was a solemn festival which lasted for eight days, and during these days baptism was solemnly conferred.[78]

Outside of these special cases in which solemn baptism was conferred in some localities on certain days, for the sake namely of attaching special importance and solemnity to particular feasts, the sacrament was universally administered only at Easter and Pentecost until about the eleventh century.

Art. 3. The Time of Baptism in Cases of Necessity

As in many of its other laws and decrees, so also in its legislation concerning the proper time of baptism, the Church in the early ages did not fail to recognize and provide for the cases of necessity that arose. Despite the fact that the Church during the first several centuries of its establishment demanded the strictest observance of its law with reference to the time of baptism, yet for prudent reasons the Church dispensed from these regulations and discharged men of their obligations whenever necessity demanded it.

Many decrees of popes and various canons of councils during

---

[76] *Epistola ad Universos Episcopos per Campanium, Samnium et Picenum Constitutos,* CLXVIII—*MPL,* LIV, 1209. JK, n. 545.

[77] Canon 3—Mansi, IX, 95.

[78] Sozomenus, *Historia Ecclesiastica,* Lib. II, c. 26: "Ex eo vero tempore solemnem quotannis festivitatem admodum splendide Hierosolymitana celebrat Ecclesia; adeo ut baptismi quoque Sacramenta eo die tradantur et per continuos octo dies collectae fiant"—*MPG,* LXVII, 1007.

these centuries made provisions relative to the cases of necessity in regard to the time for the administering of baptisms. Pope St. Leo the Great in the fifth century in his letter to the bishops of Sicily made mention of practically every kind of necessity. He allowed the laws concerning the time of baptism to be suspended in all necessities occasioned through death, sickness, persecution, attack, and shipwreck.[79] In the late fifth century Pope Gelasius (492-496) also excepted cases of necessity from his legislation concerning the time to be observed in the conferring of baptism.[80] In the ninth century Pope Nicholas I (858-867) decreed that those who are in danger of death could be baptized at any time.[81]

In addition to the decrees of the popes, several councils also granted exception in cases of necessity from the determined times for the conferring of baptism. The Council of Laodicaea (343-381) permitted that adults could be baptized at any time, in cases of emergency, but it also stated that they should later receive instructions, if they survived.[82] The Council of Gerona (517), in Spain legislated that only the infirm could be baptized on other feasts besides Easter and Pentecost.[83] Only those in danger of death were excepted from the legislation of the Synod of Auxerre (ca. 580), which stated that it was unlawful to baptize anyone outside of the Eastertide.[84] In particular, the Council of Tribur (895), in Germany, emphasized the fact that baptism could be administered at any time to those who were constituted in grave danger, since necessity hardly was governed by law.[85]

During the early centuries of the Church, death-bed baptism was considered a disqualification for the reception of sacred or-

---

[79] *Epistola IV,* c. 6: "Hi qui necessitate mortis, egritudinis, obsidionis, persecutionis, et naufragii urgentur, omni tempore debent baptizari."—JK, n. 414; *MPL,* LIV, 695; c. 16, D. IV, *de cons.*

[80] *Epistola Clero et Plebi Tarentino*—JK, n. 647; *MPL,* LIX, 137; c. 17, D. IV, *de cons.*

[81] *Responsa ad Bulgasos,* c. 69, JE, n. 2812; Mansi, XV, 425; *MPL,* CXIX, 978.

[82] Canon 47—Mansi, II, 573.

[83] Canon 5—Bruns, II, 19; C. XV, D. IV, *de cons.*

[84] Canon 18—Mansi, IX, 913.

[85] Canon 12—Mansi, XVIII, 138.

ders. So the Council of Neocaesarea, in the year 314, regulated that for anyone who had been baptized in his sick-bed it was unlawful later to receive ordination. However, in view of one's great learning and firm faith, especially when there was a lack of candidates for the priesthood, one could be admitted to holy orders.[86]

Among the Fathers of the Church, Tertullian made the statement that the conferring of baptism is not inherently confined to the feasts of Easter and Pentecost, but that any season is suitable for the giving of baptism.[87] Likewise, St. Cyprian (+258) in the third century made mention of the fact that in a case of emergency adults could be baptized at any time.[88]

In the fifth century, St. Augustine, when speaking about the specific seasons of the year for the administering of baptism, remarked that the administration of baptism was not exclusively attached to the feasts of Easter and Pentecost. He taught that necessity, no matter in what danger it arose, imposed the obligation to receive baptism on any day throughout the entire year.[89] Pope Innocent I (401-417) favored the doctrine which St. Augustine's opinion represented, and recognized the fact that in necessity the law concerning the time for the conferring of baptism was suspended. Writing on the subject, the Pope stated that every day the priest should be available, inasmuch as he could be called on to administer baptism at any time. This was one of the four reasons which the Pope offered to his priests for obliging them to celibacy.[90] Corblet claimed that Pope Innocent certainly did not want to reverse a custom universally established regarding the determined times of baptism. Rather, Corblet considered the words of Pope Innocent just one more example which clearly shows that infants and adults, in danger of death, could be baptized outside the liturgical times.[91]

---

[86] Canon 12—Mansi, II, 542; c. I, D. LVII.

[87] *De Baptismo,* XIX—*MPL,* I, 1222; CV, XX, 217.

[88] *Epistola LXXV—MPL,* IV, 413.

[89] *Sermo CCX,* C. 1, 2—*MPL,* XXXVIII, 1048.

[90] *Epistola ad Victricium Rotomagensem Episcopum,* Cap. 9—*MPL,* XX, 476, JK, n. 286.

[91] *Histoire du sacrement de baptême,* I, 476.

In the *Acts of Pope St. Stephen I* (254-257) it is recorded that, as often as persecution broke out, the bishops gathered together their people and exhorted them to receive the faith of Christ. These *Acts* bring out the fact that bishops did not wait for any special season, but baptized as soon as the danger of persecution threatened.[92] In the first centuries and in the middle ages the missionaries often could not wait for the proper seasons to baptize those whom they had converted, but frequently because of an impending danger or other necessity baptized them as soon as they were instructed.[93]

SECT. III. THE TIME OF BAPTISM IN REGARD TO THE RECIPIENT

Art. 1. The Element of Time in the Preparation of the Catechumen for Baptism

In the early Church ecclesiastical law did not allow converts to the faith to receive the grace of baptism until their sincerity in seeking baptism had been duly tested and proved after they were sufficiently instructed in the Church's doctrine. As a consequence, such converts had to go through a certain period of probation, and this period, which was called the catechumenate, was generally of long duration.

During the Apostolic ages no such periods of probation existed, inasmuch as the Church was still in its nascent stage, and had not as yet issued special legislation on particular matters. Moreover, the new converts were so zealous to join the faith that a long probationary period might have discouraged many from seeking baptism in the early days of the Church. The story of the conversion of the three thousand on the feast of Pentecost,[94] of the eunuch's conversion by Philip,[95] of the conversion of Cornelius by Peter,[96] and of the jailor's conversion at Philippi by Paul and Silas[97] are sufficient evidence that in those days the

[92] Martène, *De Antiquis Ecclesiae Ritibus,* I, 6.
[93] Corblet, *op. cit.,* I, 477.
[94] Acts, II:11-41.
[95] Acts, VIII:38.
[96] Acts, X:48.
[97] Acts, XVI:33.

catechizing of the prospective convert and the latter's reception of baptism were linked in close temporal sequence.[98]

In the succeeding ages, however, it became necessary to establish certain periods of time during which a convert underwent both a probation and instruction. Such a period was necessitated by the fact that some sought to join the Church only to satisfy an indiscreet curiosity or some other suspected motive, which demanded that persons in this stage be attentively watched and directed. To admit such curious and suspected candidates to baptism would later on terminate only in a misinterpretation of the mysteries of the faith, and perhaps in an open denunciation of Christianity. By this extended period of the catechumenate, the Church sought to eliminate from its ranks any and all vicious men who, by later becoming apostates in time of persecution, would probably jeopardize the position of the Church.

The duration of the period of preparation varied according to the custom of each church. It appeared to coincide in general with the period now called Lent.[99] In the West the Council of Elvira (305), in Spain, declared that they who are converts to the faith ought to be admitted to the sacrament of baptism within two years.[100] In the East, according to St. Gregory of Nazianzen, a catechumen had to spend three years in this stage before being admitted to baptism.[101] The I Council of Constantinople (381) spoke of such a probationary period for catechumens, but did not any more closely determine its exact duration.[102] In addition to these councils, the *Constitutiones Apostolorum* lengthened the term of probation and instruction for the catechumen to three years. Moreover, they added that converts might be admitted sooner to baptism, if they were very diligent and zealous.[103]

In Ireland the Synod of St. Patrick (456) determined that a

---

[98] Bingham, *The Antiquities of the Christian Church,* III, 444.

[99] Reichel, *A Complete Manual of Canon Law,* I, *The Sacraments* (London, 1896), p. 35.

[100] Canon 42—Mansi, II, 12; Bruns, II, 7.

[101] Oratio XL, c. 28—*MPG,* XXXVI, 400.

[102] Canon 7—Mansi, III, 563.

[103] Lib. 8, cap. 32—Funk, *Didascalia et Constitutiones Apostolorum* (2 vols., Paderbornae, 1905), I, 537.

convert to the faith had to spend at least forty days in the catechumenate.[104] According to a decree of the II Council of Braga (572) those who wished to receive baptism had to spend only a twenty-day period in the catechumenate.[105]

As regarded Jewish converts to the faith, the Council of Agde (506) decreed that they should spend a period of eight months as catechumens before they received baptism, inasmuch as they were repeatedly found to be perfidious. In a case of serious illness the Council allowed the prescribed time to be shortened.[106] But the law concerning the catechumenate of the Jews in general was somewhat elastic, so that at the end of the sixth century the duration of the catechumenate was somewhat shortened. In 598 Pope Gregory the Great (590-604), in a letter addressed to Faustinus, stated that, if the eight-month period was a hardship for a Jewish convert, then it was permissible to commute the time of the catechumenate to forty days. After these forty days of fast, they could be baptized.[107]

(A) The extension of the catechumenate

In some particular cases, when it was evident that a catechumen had been guilty of a grave fault or of conduct unbecoming to a Christian, it was customary to prolong the time of probation.[108] It is clear that such an extension of the time of probation served as a form of punishment. The catechumenate, besides being prolonged, could also be prolonged in the case of a candidate who at the termination of the established time had only a vague or an insufficient knowledge of the doctrine of the Church. Some converts were often so imbued with the pagan teachings of the philosophers and so attached to pagan rites and ceremonies, that it was only slowly and with the greatest difficulty that they could be instructed in the true faith. For such people, then, it was necessary that the Church insist on a greater duration in the cate-

[104] Canon 29—Bruns, II, 304.

[105] Canon 1—Bruns, II, 39; c. 55, D. IV, *de cons.*

[106] Canon 34—Bruns, II, 153; c. 93, D. IV, *de cons.*

[107] C. 98, D. IV, *de cons.;* JE, n. 1511.

[108] Corblet, *Histoire de sacrement de baptême*, I, 452.

chumenate and on a more sustained probation, before they could be admitted to the Church through baptism.

As a consequence of all this, the Council of Elvira (305) prorogued the time of the catechumenate from two to three years as punishment for those catechumens who assumed the priestly office of a heathen flamen, even though they did not offer sacrifice.[109] Likewise, this Council punished any woman catechumen who remarried when her husband had left her, or who married a man who already had a wife, by prolonging the time of her probation to five years.[110] Furthermore, in another canon this same Council severely punished any woman who committed adultery, or who perpetrated an abortion, by lengthening the time of the catechumenate to the end of her life, and baptizing her only at the time of death.[111]

(B) The curtailment of the period of the catechumenate

There were occasions when the time of the catechumenate was shortened either on account of urgent necessity or in view of an extant danger of death. Such a foreshortening of the time fell also to the benefit of those catechumens who through their outstanding talents and ability had more readily than the others acquired a clear concept of the Church's doctrine and a full grasp of its vital practice. In addition to these cases, the time of the catechumenate was also shortened in consequence of the variously modifying circumstances that obtained in the different localities.

Missionaries, in the early ages, could not impose long periods of time on those whom they converted by their words or miracles. Many of the first apostles in Northern Europe baptized numerous populations, after only a few days of instruction.[112] As regards the curtailment of the time of the catechumenate, Socrates (ca. 380-ca. 450), in his *Ecclesiastical History,* observed that in the

[109] Canon 4—Bruns, II, 2; Mansi, II, 6.
[110] Canon 11—Bruns, II, 3; Mansi, II, 6.
[111] Canon 68—Mansi, II, 14; Bruns, II, 11.
[112] Corblet, *Histoire du sacrement de baptême,* I, 452.

conversion of the Burgundians the French bishops held them only to a period of seven days for the catechumenate, and on the eighth day baptized them.[113]

Although the baptism of a catechumen had been deferred for one or several years or even until the end of his life, he could upon an express desire for it always receive baptism at the hour of death. Likewise, baptism was immediately conferred also on those catechumens who in the midst of the period of their probation were found to be in danger of death. In one of his epistles, St. Cyril of Alexandria (ca. 376-444) ordered that catechumens whose baptism had been deferred on account of their lapse into grave sin were to be baptized at the hour of death, lest they leave this life without becoming partakers of grace.[114] Epiphanius of Salamis (315-403) made the observation that all catechumens who were in the danger of death were always admitted to baptism.[115]

(C) The indefinite delay of the reception of baptism

Although there were occasions in which the period of the catechumenate was shortened, yet in the early ages there were many people who, notwithstanding their conviction concerning the faith, voluntarily deferred baptism for an indefinite period, or even until the end of their life. This practice of deferring baptism indefinitely was against the rule of the Church, and there are numerous complaints in the writings of the Fathers against those who were guilty of this practice. Of course, several supposedly acceptable reasons were alleged for such a delay, and it was one or the other of these excuses that procrastinators offered in their defense. Some alleged the fear of falling from grace after baptism; others, an unwillingness to assume the grave responsibilities of a Christian and to submit to the discipline of the Church; still others acted on the pretense of following the example of Christ, Who was not baptized until He was thirty years of age.

[113] Lib. 7, cap. 30—*MPG,* LXVII, 806.

[114] *Epistola LXXIX ad Episcopos in Libya et Pentapoli—MPG,* LXXVII, 363.

[115] *Adversus Haereses,* Lib. 1, Haers. 28, n. 6—*MPG,* XLI, 386.

Against those who deferred baptism because of their unwillingness to accept the severities of the faith, St. Gregory of Nazianzen openly denounced their motive as part of a pagan philosophy.[116]

Those who pretended to have great fear of lapsing again into sin after they had received baptism often preferred to defer baptism until the hour of death. They hoped thus to enter immediately into heaven, having through baptism been completely cleansed of all stain of sin. As a defense for their delay of baptism, such people could well offer the words of Tertullian, who declared that in view of the grave responsibilities assumed in baptism one had more to fear from these consequences than from the delay of baptism itself.[117] Indeed, it was precisely in consideration of this statement that many people procrastinated their baptism from day to day.

Speaking against these people, St. Gregory of Nyssa called their excuses a specious pretext of timidity. He said they feared baptism not so much because they might lose its grace, but because it prohibited to them certain pleasures and made them abstain from evil delights.[118] In like manner, St. Basil stressed the factor of the uncertainty of life for all those who delayed their reception of baptism in the fear of losing their newly gained baptismal innocence.[119]

The pretense of those who procrastinated their baptism to the age of thirty, for the reason that Christ Himself did not receive baptism until He had reached that age, was refuted by St. Gregory of Nazianzen. He stated that Christ, as God, did not need baptism, and that under such a consideration no evil could befall Him in consequence of any delay in the reception of baptism.[120]

From the writings of the Fathers, therefore, one can well draw the conclusion that baptism was not to be delayed in view of these pretended excuses. Only for two reasons could baptism be de-

[116] *Oratio XL (De Baptismo)—MPG,* XXXVI, 394.

[117] *De Baptismo,* Cap. 4—*MPL,* 1, 1311; *CV,* XX, 203.

[118] *Adversus eos qui baptismum differunt—MPG,* XLIV, 415.

[119] *Homilia exhortatoria ad sanctum baptismum,* V—*MPG,* XXXI, 434.

[120] *Oratio XL (in Sanctum Lavacrum),* CXXXIX—*MPG,* XXXVI, 399.

ferred. One was the need of the candidate's fuller instruction in the doctrines of the Church, which instruction took place in the period of the catechumenate. The other was the punishment that was to be undergone by a catechumen who clung to a sinful habit, which punishment consisted in the fact that baptism was denied for a time.

At the advent of the middle ages most of the people in Central and Southern Europe were ready to embrace the faith. Conversions had so multiplied that people entered the Church in large groups, and as a consequence the intimate probation of candidates became difficult and sometimes impossible. More and more the bishops had to curtail the period of the catechumenate, until they finally dispensed from it in many cases.

As time went on, the catechumenate was reduced more and more to the preparation immediately preceding the baptism of adults. A sustained period of probation became the exception. Thus, many of the laws that governed the catechumenate, especially those concerning its duration, passed into oblivion.[121]

Art. 2. The Baptism of Infants

In the Gospels there is not any text which explicitly states that infants must be baptized, but the need of baptism on their part is implicit in the text: "Unless a man be born again of water and the Holy Ghost, he cannot enter into the kingdom of God."[122] The word *quis* as used in the Latin text comprehends every member of the human race, young and old, and is not limited in its extension in such a manner as to include only those who are adults. For if this term were applicable only to adults and not to infants, it would be implied that infants are not capable of salvation, since they are not capable of baptism.[123]

Since its establishment by Christ, the Church has always practiced infant baptism.[124] It is true that it is not explicitly stated

---

[121] Bareille, "Catechumenat," *DTC*, II, 1974.

[122] John, III:5.

[123] Kenrick, *A Treatise on Baptism* (Baltimore, 1852), p. 125.

[124] Bareille, "Baptême d'apres les Pères Grecs et Latins," *DTC*, II, 192.

in the *Acts* and the *Epistles* that the Apostles baptized infants, but that can be inferred from the texts. Speaking of a certain woman named Lydia, the *Acts of the Apostles* relate that she and her whole household had been baptized.[125] Again, in the same chapter it is related that Paul and Silas baptized the prison guard and his whole household.[126] Likewise, St. Paul in his *First Epistle to the Corinthians* testified that he baptized the household of Stephanus.[127] None of these texts gives positive evidence that there were infants in these households, but there is a strong presumption that if there were infants in them they likewise shared in the conversion of the parents.[128]

From the second century onward both the Fathers and the councils treat of infant baptism. Among the first of the Fathers, St. Justin Martyr (ca. 167) stated that in his time there were older persons of both sexes who had been Christians from their infancy.[129] Since Justin wrote his apology about the middle of the second century, those older persons of sixty or seventy of whom he spoke must have been born toward the end of the Apostolic age.

In the same century there is the first direct evidence of infant baptism. It comes from St. Irenaeus (130-203), who was a disciple of St. Polycarp (+155/156), who in turn had been a disciple of St. John. Irenaeus stated that Our Lord came into this world in order that He might save all. Since infants are under the guilt of original sin, he said they also share in this universal salvation.[130] Origen (185-254) offered very clear testimony regarding the fact that the baptism of infants was not only a recognized practice of the Church in his day, but that it was of Apostolic tradition.[131] In another place he said that everyone

---

[125] Acts, XVI:15.
[126] Acts, XVI:33.
[127] I Cor., I:16.
[128] Kenrick, *op. cit.*, p. 131.
[129] *Apologia II pro Christianis*, Cap. I—*MPG*, VI, 442.
[130] *Contra Haereses*, Lib. II, c. 22—*MPG*, VII, 784.
[131] *Epistola ad Romanos*, Lib. V, c. 6—*MPG*, XIV, 1052.

was born in original sin, and that therefore baptism, which grants the remission of sin, needs to be given even to infants.[132]

Tertullian (ca. 155-ca. 235), it is true, argued against the practice of infant baptism,[133] but his statements did not deny the existence of the practice. Rather, he offered clear proof that it was the custom of the early Church to baptize infants. His arguments against infant baptism, however, reflected his own private opinion, and seemed to indicate that he was seeking to make an innovation in contrast to the Church's current practice of baptizing infants.[134] In proposing his opinion, he had the purpose of guarding against the general danger in which were placed such sponsors as did not fulfill their promises, or as might have been deceived in the event of any future misconduct on the part of the baptized. In his work, so it is commonly believed, he was speaking of the children of unbelievers.[135] Nevertheless, Tertullian did plead for the baptism of infants in danger of death, and furthermore he did not doubt concerning the validity of baptism administered to infants, even in the cases wherein such danger did not exist.[136]

In the middle of the third century St. Cyprian (+258) testified concerning the baptism of infants in his response to Fidus, an African bishop. Fidus had asked if infants could be baptized within the second or third day after birth, or if they had to wait until the eighth day, as in the case of circumcision. To this question Cyprian and a group of six bishops, gathered in a Council of Carthage, clearly asserted that baptism can not be denied to anyone born into this world.[137]

St. Ambrose (+ 397) recommended that an infant be baptized on the eighth day after birth, not because of any necessity, but for reasons of special significance.[138] St. Augustine (354-430)

---

[132] *Homilia 8 in Levit.—MPG,* XII, 496.

[133] *De Baptismo,* Cap. 18—*MPL,* I, 1220; *CV,* XX, 215.

[134] Bingham, *The Antiquities of the Christian Church,* IV, 62.

[135] Risi, *De Baptismo Parvulorum in Primitiva Ecclesia* (Romae, 1870), p. 27.

[136] Kenrick, *op. cit.,* p. 141.

[137] *Epistola 59 (ad Fidum)—MPL,* IV, 559.

[138] *Ep. XLIV (ad Horontianum)—MPL,* XVI, 1137.

likewise testified that the practice of the Church in baptizing infants was of Apostolic tradition.[139] In the fifth century St. Jerome (+420) gave further evidence that the baptism of infants was the practice of his day.[140]

From the opinion as here represented, St. Gregory of Nazianzen deviated. Because of this fact his opinion is quite singular among the Fathers of the Church, and it never gained any esteem in the public practice of the Church. He thought that outside the danger of death it was better to defer baptism until the child was about three years old, when there could emerge some understanding of the doctrines of the faith, and a request be made for baptism.[141]

In addition to the Fathers in their writings, Pope Siricius in the year 385 also mentioned the baptism of infants in one of his epistles. He clearly indicated that infants should be baptized without delay, and in his statement he placed them in the same category as those who were in necessity.[142]

Among the councils which treated of the baptism of infants, the Council of Carthage which was held in 418 ranks high in importance. It assailed the Pelagians and other heretics who denied the baptism of infants. Since the practice of infant baptism always existed in the Church, this council anathematized all who condemned infant baptism, or who denied that it was conferred for the remission of sin.[143] In the canons of the II Council of Braga (572),[144] the Synod of Auxerre (ca. 580),[145] and the II Council of Mâcon (585),[146] there is incontrovertible evidence that the baptism of infants stood approved, as may be seen from the conciliar enactments.

---

[139] *De Genesi ad litteram,* Lib. X, c. 23—*MPL,* XXXIV, 426. *De peccatorum meritis et remissione,* Lib. I, c. 26—*MPL,* XLIV, 131.

[140] *Dialogus adversus Pelagianos,* Lib. III, c. 18: "Et a baptismo atque gratia nemo prohibetur, quanto magis prohiberi non debet infans, qui recens natus nihil peccavit."—*MPL,* XXIII, 5888.

[141] *Oratio XL (in Sanctum Lavacrum),* CXXXIX, MPG, XXXVI, 399.

[142] *Epistola ad Himerium,* c. II—*MPL,* XIII, 1134.

[143] Canon 2—Mansi, IV, 327.

[144] Canon 9—Bruns, II, 42.

[145] Canon 18—Mansi, IX, 913.

[146] Canon 3—Mansi, IX, 951.

At the end of the seventh century an Anglo-Saxon Council (692), convened by King Ina, legislated that children were to be baptized within thirty days of their birth; otherwise the parents were to pay a fine.[147] About a century later, in the year 782, Charlemagne enacted a statute that all infants were to be baptized within a year of their birth. If after a year they still remained unbaptized without the permission of a priest, then the father was to pay a fine.[148]

In 967 King Edgar (959-975), in his ecclesiastical laws for the Saxons, stated that every infant was to be baptized within thirty-seven days of its birth.[149] Again, about three centuries later, the Council of Reading (1279) in England, convened by John Peckham, Archbishop of Canterbury (1279-1292), enacted particular legislation concerning the baptism of infants. It decreed that if a child was born within eight days before Easter or Pentecost, and was not in danger of death, its baptism was to be reserved until the vigil of Easter or of Pentecost. Others, however, who were born outside that time, or who were in danger of death, were to be baptized without delay.[150] Hugo of St. Victor (1096-1141) taught that infants were to be admitted to the sacrament of baptism, inasmuch as the Church supplied what was lacking in them until they arrived at the age when they could understand the significance of the sacraments.[151] Innocent III (1198-1216) in a letter to the Archbishop of Arles in 1201 stated that care was to be taken in order that infants, of whom so many day by day died, would not perish without baptism.[152] St. Thomas

[147] Canon 2—Mansi, XII, 57.

[148] *Capitularia Caroli Magni* (Pars I, Sect. I, n. 19—*MPL,* XCVII, 147; *MGH, Leges in 4,* Sectio II (*Capitularia Regum Francorum*), I (ed. A. Boretius, 1883), 69.

[149] Canon 15—Mansi, XVIII, 515.

[150] Constitutio 4—Labbé-Cossart, *Sacrosancta Concilia ad regiam Editionem Exacta* (15 vols. in 16, Paris, 1671-1674), XI, 1068 (hereafter cited as Labbé).

[151] *De Sacramentis,* Lib. II, p. VI, c. 9—*MPL,* CLXXVI, 456.

[152] Denzinger-Bannwart-Umberg, *Enchiridion Symbolorum et Definitionum de Rebus Fidei et Morum* (editio 21.-23., Friburgi Brisgoviae: Herder and Co., 1937), n. 410.

Aquinas (1225-1274) stated that the baptism of infants was not to be deferred, especially in view of the attendant great danger of death, since there was no other means for their eternal salvation than the sacrament of baptism.[153]

In the Council of Vienna (1311), convened under Pope Clement V (1305-1314), it was declared that baptism existed both for adults and for infants, and stood as a perfect means for the gaining of eternal salvation.[154] About forty years later, in 1351, Clement VI (1342-1352) clearly stated that children could be baptized before the eighth day after birth.[155] In a constitution of the Council of Florence (1439-1445) Eugene IV (1431-1447) clearly warned that the baptism of children was not to be deferred until the eightieth or fortieth day after birth, but that baptism ought to be conferred as soon as possible. In the same constitution he added that those children who were in a proximate danger of death were to be baptized without any delay.[156] Shortly before the Council of Trent, the Council of Sens (1528) solemnly condemned the error that infants were not to be baptized.[157]

Through the foregoing outline of the statements of the various Fathers, and of the declarations of some of the popes and the councils from Apostolic times to the Council of Trent, it is evident that the administration of infant baptism has been the practice of the Church since early times. Moreover, it has also been the practice to baptize infants within a short period after birth, and thus Pope Eugene IV, in the Council of Florence, made it a universal law of the Church that all infants were to be baptized *quamprimum*.

---

[153] *Summa Theologica,* Pars III, q. LXVIII, a. 3.

[154] Council of Vienne—Mansi, XXV, 411.

[155] Ep. *Super quibusdam,* 29 sept. 1351—*Codicis Iuris Canonici Fontes* (curâ Emi Petri Card Gasparri editi, 9 vols., Romae, 1923-1939) (Vols. VII, VIII et IX, ed. cura et studio Emi Iustiniani Card. Serédi), n. 42 (hereafter referred to as *Fontes*).

[156] Const. *Cantate Domino,* 4 febr. 1441—*Fontes,* n. 54.

[157] Canon 10—Labbé, XIV, 468.

CHAPTER II

The Place of Baptism From the Apostolic Age to the Council of Trent

SECT. 1. BAPTISM IN RIVERS, STREAMS, AND FOUNTAINS

During and especially after the time of the Apostles the Church was tormented on all sides with hatreds and persecutions. As a consequence, the Church celebrated the divine services and conferred the sacraments in private, and often in a very secret manner. Such conditions naturally kept the followers of Christ from erecting even the simplest permanent edifice for the performance of the rites of the ceremony of baptism. The Church, therefore, following the example of Christ, used the most convenient, yet truly suitable, places to confer the sacrament, by conferring baptism in rivers, brooks, lakes, fountains, and seas.

Moreover, baptism in the early Church was conferred by way of immersion. This form of baptism required a large pool or font for the administering of the sacrament to the large number of converts that existed in those days. In the absence of oratories with baptismal fonts, the Church adapted itself to the more difficult conditions of the employment of rivers, lakes and fonts as places for the giving of baptism.

Among the early writings, the *Didache* or *Teaching of the Twelve Apostles* instructed the ministers of the sacraments to confer the sacrament of baptism in running water.[1] The heading of this instruction reflects the practice of the early Christians, who administered the sacrament of baptism in waters of springs and flowing rivers.[2]

In like manner St. Justin taught that those who wished to do penance and to receive baptism were to be brought to a place

[1] Sabatier, *La Didache* (Paris, 1885), p. 52.

[2] *The Apostolic Fathers,* translated by F. Glimm, J. Marique, and G. Walsh (New York: Cima Publishing Co., 1947), p. 177, ft. 3.

where there was water.[3] Concerning the place of baptism, Tertullian said that it was not a matter of difference whether a person was washed in the sea, in a pool, in a river, in a spring, or in a lake. He further stated that all waters obtained the mystery of sanctification after God has been invoked.[4]

In the fourth and fifth centuries, baptism in rivers and streams became a rare practice almost everywhere, for by that time churches and baptisteries had been established in most of the regions to which Christianity had spread.[5] As late as the seventh century St. Paulinus, one of the bishops sent with St. Augustine (+605) to England by Gregory I, is said still to have conferred baptism to several thousands of Northumbrian converts in the rivers Glen, Trent and Swales.[6] From the eighth to the twelfth centuries, baptism by immersion in rivers was most exceptional, and was practiced only in missionary territory.[7]

Thus in the progress of time the practice of baptizing in rivers, streams, or fountains either disappeared where some form of permanent baptisteries was established, and there were fewer candidates to be baptized, or it was forbidden by ecclesiastical legislation. It was allowed only on the occasion of extreme necessity, or in pagan countries where it was still necessary to baptize large crowds.

SECT. II. BAPTISM IN PRIVATE HOMES AND ORATORIES

Since the time fixed by the Church for solemn baptism was the season of Easter, it was often too cold during this period to administer baptism in rivers, fonts and springs. Only too often did the catechumens find it a hardship to submit to the immersions in such cold waters. Moreover, it was most difficult in these circumstances to observe the rules of decency, since a catechumen,

---

[3] *Apologia I pro Christianis,* Cap. 61—*MPG,* VI, 422.

[4] *De Baptismo,* Cap. 2—*MPL,* I, 1201; *CV,* XX, 201.

[5] Corblet, *Histoire du sacrement de baptême,* II, 3.

[6] Beda Venerabilis (673-735), *Historia Ecclesiastica,* Lib. 2, c. 14—*MPL,* XCV, 106.

[7] Corblet, *op. cit.,* II, 3.

according to the ritual, was divested of his or her garments before being immersed in the water.[8]

In consideration of these facts, the early Christians were soon compelled to withdraw within some enclosure, both for protection against the cold weather, and for the preservation of decency. The first fixed baptisteries were, therefore, not in churches but in the private homes of the Romans.[9] In its arrangement the Roman house could well be adapted for the administration of the sacrament of baptism. In nearly all the larger Roman houses there was an atrium in which the center part of the roof was opened to the sky. Through this center opening the rain fell into a basin, called the *impluvium,* which was situated in the center of the atrium. The catechumens descended into this *impluvium,* where entirely or partly immersed they were baptized.[10] If a house was of a less elaborate plan, then the bath-chamber, which most Roman houses possessed, served as a fitting place for the conferring of baptism.[11]

Thus during the times of the persecutions, when the Christians had to worship secretly and could not build churches, the private homes of some of them served very well as private oratories. Because the homes were large and elaborate, they could easily be converted and advantageously made to serve the Christians, especially in the administration of baptism.

After the conversion of Constantine, the Christians began to erect churches, and they were no longer permitted to confer baptism in their homes. There was only one exception to this law which was made in favor of those who, as a result of sickness, had to remain in bed. In 692 the Council in Trullo legislated that baptism was never to be administered in an oratory. Instead, they who were considered worthy of baptism were to go to their church to receive the sacrament. If a cleric did not observe this law, the Council enacted that he was to be deposed, and a layman ex-

---

[8] Corblet, *Histoire du sacrement de baptême,* II, 11.

[9] Goettelmann, *The Baptistery of Frejus* (Washington, D. C.: The Catholic University of America, 1933), p. 2.

[10] Corblet, *op. cit.,* II, 169.

[11] Goettelmann, *op. cit.,* p. 2.

communicated.[12] Likewise the Council of Meaux, in 845, stated that it was forbidden to administer baptism in a private house.[13] The Council of Tribur (895), in Germany, allowed the sick who could not be brought to church to be baptized in a decent place, especially in their homes.[14]

In England, in 1236, it was decreed that if a child had been baptized by a layman at home, the water that was used in the baptism was either to be thrown into the fire or carried to the church in order to be poured into the baptistery. Moreover, the vessel in which the baptism was performed was to be burnt or deputed to the use of the Church.[15]

Pope Clement V, in the Council of Vienne (1311), firmly prohibited the administration of solemn baptism in halls, chambers, or private houses. He stated that the church, in which the baptismal font was located, was the proper place of baptism. To this law he allowed two exceptions. The children of kings or rulers of a country could be solemnly baptized at home, if they freely asked for this. Likewise in a case of necessity in which a child could not be brought to church without danger to his health, he could be solemnly baptized at home. Those who presumed to violate this law were to be punished by the bishop.[16]

SECT. III. THE BAPTISTERIES

After the cessation of the persecutions and following the conversion of Constantine, the Church had such a glorious triumph that the Christians no longer had to worship secretly in the privacy of their homes or catacombs. Soon they began to construct churches and spacious buildings for the administration of baptism.[17] From the primitive baptisteries in the Roman homes and catacombs, there was but one step to the erection of these baptisteries during the time of Constantine. Often enough the early

---

[12] Canon 59—Mansi, XI, 970.

[13] Canon 48—Mansi, XIV, 830.

[14] Canon 12—Mansi, XVIII, 138.

[15] *Constitutiones Provinciales Edmundi Rich,* Const. 10—*Mansi,* XXIII, 416.

[16] C. un., *de baptismo et eius effectu,* III, 15, in Clem.

[17] Martigny, *Dictionnaire des Antiquités Chrétiennes,* p. 72.

Christians merely converted small pagan temples or mausoleums into baptisteries. At other times they erected completely new buildings for the purpose of administering baptism.[18]

Originally the baptistery was outside the church and completely detached from it, but yet within the boundaries of the church property. Bingham mentioned the fact that Eusebius (263-339), in speaking of the church of a certain Paulinus at Tyre, primarily included the baptistery among the buildings outside the church.[19] Paulinus (353-431), Bishop of Nola (409-431), said that his friend, Severus, built a baptistery between two churches.[20] Again, St. Cyril of Jerusalem (ca. 315-386) described the baptistery as a building which was completely detached from the church, and in which there was a porch or ante-room. Into this porch the catechumens entered and made their renunciation of Satan and their confession of faith.[21]

The separation of the baptistery from the church was not without purpose. Before the conversion of Constantine, the sacrament of baptism was conferred in the atrium of the home where there was a large basin or bath very suitable for the conferring of baptism, which was at that time administered in the form of immersion.

Since baptism was conferred by way of immersion, a large receptacle for the water was naturally required. Besides, baptism was conferred only in the seasons of Easter and Pentecost in the early ages of the Church, and large crowds of people assembled during these seasons. In consideration both of the fact of immersion, and of the large concourse of people, there was need of large rooms and apartments in which baptism might be administered.

The churches of the early Christians were quite small and were easily filled for divine services. As a consequence of this fact, the

---

[18] Leclercq, *Baptistère—Dictionnaire d'archéologie chrétienne et de liturgie* (15 vols., incomplete, Paris, 1907—), II, 390; Goettelmann, *The Baptistery of Frejus,* p. 6.

[19] *The Antiquities of the Christian Church,* III, 117.

[20] *Epistola 12* (ad Severum)—*MPL,* LXI, 200.

[21] *Catechesis,* Mystagogica, 1, n. 2—*MPG,* XXXIII, 570.

presence of the *piscina* or large receptacle for water in the church somewhat limited the space allowed for a congregation in an already overcrowded church. To eliminate the resulting hardship and to allow space for all those who were to receive baptism during these feasts, the erection of a large edifice, detached from the church, was required for the administration of baptism. Moreover, the early Christians had a deep respect for the house of God, and were very reluctant to allow a vast number of catechumens, upon whom were performed the ceremonies of exorcism, to enter the church. To them it seemed more fitting to perform these ceremonies, preparatory to the sacrament of baptism, in a place annexed to the church. Thus from these circumstances the practice of constructing a building distinct from the church or basilica very naturally arose.[22]

Because of the fact that baptism was conferred only at two or three times in the year, and since a great multitude of people was generally baptized on these occasions, there were often several baptismal fonts in the same baptistery. Sometimes, in the first centuries of the Church, the multitude who came to be baptized numbered several thousands.[23]

SECT. IV. BAPTISMAL FONTS

The practice of erecting an edifice, separated from the church, to serve as a baptistery was observed up to the sixth century. After that period Christians began to discard the practice of building baptisteries, and in place of them, they erected baptismal fonts in the church, at first in the *narthex* and finally in the interior of the church.[24] Corblet claimed that this change from a separate baptistery to a simple baptismal font within the church was made, because it was found inconvenient to have a baptistery separate from the church. According to this author, the baptismal font was first erected in the center of the atrium of the basilica or at the extremity of the *narthex,* ordinarily on the right, and it

---

[22] Smith and Cheetham, *Dictionary of Christian Antiquities,* I, 174; Leclercq, "Baptistère," *Dictionnaire d'archéologie chrétienne et de liturgie,* II, 390.

[23] Martène, *De Antiquis Ecclesiae Ritibus,* I, 11.

[24] Martigny, *Dictionnaire des Antiquités Chrétiennes,* p. 73.

was only in the seventh century that the baptismal font was erected within the interior of the church.[25]

Relative to its purpose, this change was motivated not so much in consequence of the factor of inconvenience, as by the fact that the number of adult candidates for baptism greatly declined, and the baptism of children became general. The *piscina* found in the early baptisteries was very large in accommodation of the large number of adults who received baptism at the two established seasons of the year. When the baptism of children became general in the eighth century, many of the baptisteries lost their essential purpose; however, the baptisteries were left standing, the *piscina* being covered over, and a baptismal font being erected in its place.[26]

The Constitutions of St. Edmund of Canterbury (1236) decreed that the baptismal font should be made of stone.[27] In the Capitularies of Hincmar (806-882), Archbishop of Reims (845-882), as cited by Gratian, it was stated that every priest, if he could not have a stone font, should at least have a special vessel for the purpose of baptizing. Furthermore the Capitularies legislated that the vessel could not be taken outside the church.[28]

St. Ildefonsus, Archbishop of Toledo (657-667) said that the baptismal font was closed and sealed with the episcopal ring at the beginning of Lent, and was opened at Easter with the blessing of the priest. Only in the most grave necessity was it ever allowed to open the baptismal font during the time of Lent.[29] The Constitutions of St. Edmund legislated also that baptismal fonts were to be locked securely, and that the chrism and holy oil were to be kept in a safely guarded place. There was attached to this law a three months' suspension from office for anyone who was negligent in his duty in regard to the custody of the baptismal font and the holy oils.[30]

---

[25] *Histoire du sacrement de baptême,* II, 13.

[26] Leclercq, "Baptistère," *Dictionnaire d'archéologie chrétienne et de liturgie,* II, 391; Goettelmann, *The Baptistery of Frejus,* p. 8.

[27] Const. 10—Mansi, XXIII, 419.

[28] Cap. 3—Mansi, XV, 476; c. 106, D. IV, *de cons.*

[29] *De cognitione baptismi,* Lib. I, c. 107—*MPL,* XCVI, 156.

[30] Const. 9—Mansi, XXIII, 419.

SECT. V. BAPTISMAL CHURCHES

Art. 1. Origin and Development

In the first centuries of the Church it was the right of the bishop alone to administer baptism. As a consequence of this practice, baptisteries were attached only to the cathedral church, and thus baptism was conferred only in the church where the bishop resided.[31] Moreover, in those times the bishop's parish and the diocese were identical, so that the bishop was the sole pastor over all his diocesan territory. The bishopric was called a *paroecia,* and the administration of the sacraments was completely in the hands of the bishop. Only with a special mandate from the bishop in a particular case could a priest administer baptism and the other sacraments.

It was in the East that the development of parish organization first became evident.[32] When the Christians began to increase in large numbers, the cathedral church became insufficient for satisfying the spiritual needs of the faithful. Likewise the bishop found himself greatly incompetent to care for such a multitude over so large a territory. The idea of chor-episcopi, who were assistants to the bishop, was disapproved of by the Church, and the system of having the priests go around in the name of the bishop was not sufficient. Thus the result was that a number of chapels and oratories were erected in the rural districts, and these were served by priests and deacons who were previously assistants in the bishop's parish.[33]

As these rural oratories and chapels began to increase in number in the East, priests received permission much more frequently

---

[31] Torquebiau, "Baptême en Occident," *Dictionnaire de Droit Canonique* (4 vols. and 2 fascicles, Paris: Letouzey et Ané, 1924—), II, 165; Martène, *De Antiquis Ritibus Ecclesiae,* I, 12.

[32] Nicholas Connolly, *The Canonical Erection of Parishes,* The Catholic University of America Canon Law Studies, n. 114 (Washington, D. C.: The Catholic University of America, 1938), p. 16.

[33] Corblet, *Histoire du sacrement de baptême,* II, 83.

to administer the sacraments.[34] Permission was conceded for some rural churches to have baptisteries. Baptism was not administered in all rural churches, but only in those churches which were selected for that purpose. These were called baptismal churches and were under the supervision of an archpriest.[35]

In the West the establishment of baptismal churches came somewhat later than in the East. Rome was an exception to this practice. At the very beginning of the second century, Pope St. Evaristus (97-105) formed a quasi-parochial system by dividing *titles* in the city of Rome among the priests.[36]

Later Pope Dionysius (259-268) is said to have divided the churches among priests and to have given these churches definite parish boundaries. The priests had the care of souls within these boundaries. This claim, however, is based on a document of doubtful authority.[37] Again, in the fourth century, Pope Marcellus (308-309) made a new division of the city of Rome by constituting twenty-five titles for the purpose of administering baptism and penance.[38]

Imbart de la Taur (1860-1925) stated that in the Merovingian age, which commenced with the reign of King Clovis (481-511), there were two types of churches. One of these had a baptistery, and in it Mass was publicly celebrated. In the city this was the church of the bishop or the *ecclesia mater*. The other type of church was a chapel which neither possessed nor had any boundaries attached to it. This same division of churches was also observed in the Carolingian period, so that the parish church had the care of souls within a certain district, while the chapel was located within the parish boundaries and was subject to the parish church.[39]

Although Thomassinus (1619-1695) stated that baptismal

---

[34] Thomassinus, *Vetus et Nova Ecclesiae Disciplina* (3 vols., Parisiis, 1688), Pars I, Lib. II, cap. 23, n. 12.

[35] Thomassinus, *op. cit.*, Pars I, Lib. II, cap. 5, n. 8.

[36] *Liber Pontificalis,* In Vita Evaristi Papae—Mansi, I, 621.

[37] *Liber Pontificalis,* Ep. I Dionysii ad Severum—Mansi, I, 1006.

[38] *Liber Pontificalis,* In Vita Marcelli Papae—Mansi, I, 1259.

[39] *De Ecclesiis Rusticanis Aetate Carolingica* (Parisiis, 1890), p. 4.

churches were under the direction of an archpriest,[40] yet Imbart de la Tour maintained that it cannot be proved that in France, during the Carolingian period, baptism was administered only in the church of the archpriest. Rather, he claimed that all churches were baptismal churches if they contained a baptistery, whether the church was under the supervision of an archpriest or not.[41]

In Spain the existence of baptismal churches as early as the sixth century is established.[42] In Italy, outside of Rome, baptismal churches were established about the same time as in France, which was around the beginning of the sixth century.[43]

In Germany the evolution of parishes was slower than in France. Inasmuch as the baptismal churches were not numerous, their boundaries embraced extensive territory. The archpriest was the pastor of the baptismal church. Since the office of archpriest was instituted in Germany during the ninth to the eleventh centuries, baptismal churches must have been in existence in that country at least by the tenth century.[44] A few maintain that baptismal churches were not established in Germany until the eleventh century.[45]

Until the eighth century there was only one parish church in the urban district, and that was the espiscopal church, which served the needs of all who lived within the boundaries of the city. This was the case in every city with the exception of Alexandria and Antioch in the East, and Rome in the West. When the population in the major cities began to increase, the bishops found their cathedral church inadequate to care for all the faithful in the urban district. As a consequence, the bishops erected a few churches around the cathedral and gave their priests the right to baptize. At first the bishops retained some parochial rights other

---

[40] *Vetus et Nova Ecclesiae Disciplina,* Pars I, Lib. II, cap. 23, n. 12.

[41] *Op. cit.,* p. 8.

[42] II Council of Braga (572), canon 2—Bruns, II, 40.

[43] Kurtscheid, *Historia Iuris Canonici, Historia Institutorum,* Vol. I (*ab Ecclesiae Fundatione usque ad Gratianum*) (Romae: Officium Libri Catholici, 1941), p. 277.

[44] Kurtscheid, *op. cit.,* p. 264.

[45] Torquebiau, "Baptême en Occident," *Dictionnaire de Droit Canonique,* II, 166.

than baptism for the cathedral church, but little by little the baptismal churches acquired all parochial rights, so that they became true parochial churches. This practice, which was somewhat restricted in the eighth and ninth centuries, became universal from the tenth to the twelfth centuries.[46] Thus by the twelfth century the system of baptismal churches, which were the forerunners of the parish churches, was firmly established in both the rural and urban districts in the East and the West.

Art. 2. The Peculiar Rights of Baptismal Churches

It was an essential right of the baptismal churches to confer baptism on all the infants and adults who lived within a certain determined area surrounding the church. It is more generally believed that in those days an infant or adult candidate could be baptized in the baptismal church of the district where the child's father or the adult himself had a domicile or quasi-domicile, or even in the baptismal church of the place where these persons happened to be dwelling for a short time.[47]

Several councils made explicit mention of baptismal churches. During a council assembled in Verneuil in 755, it was decreed that a public baptistery was to be erected only in those churches which the bishop specially constituted. Only in case of sickness or of some other necessity did the priests have the permission of conferring baptism in some other place, so that no one might die without baptism.[48] In 845 the Council of Meaux legislated that no priest was to presume to baptize anybody unless the baptism was administered in a baptismal church.[49] In the Ecclesiastical Law of King Edgar (967) it was also stated that no priest could baptize outside the baptismal church.[50] The Council of Limoges (1032) made similar legislation concerning baptismal churches.[51] Gratian stated that a Council of Toledo, of uncertain date, legis-

---

[46] Kurtscheid, *op. cit.*, p. 282.

[47] Corblet, *Histoire du sacrement de baptême*, II, 86.

[48] Canon 7—Mansi, XII, 581.

[49] Canon 48—Mansi, XIV, 830.

[50] Canon 15—Mansi, XVIII, 515.

[51] Sessio II—Mansi, XIX, 543.

lated that there could not be several baptismal churches in the same district.[52]

In the Ambrosian rite the baptismal fonts were not blessed in the baptismal churches at Easter and Pentecost. This blessing was given only in the cathedral church, and the priests of the baptismal churches had to come to the cathedral and carry baptismal water in procession to their churches.[53] Gratian stated that Pope Gregory I (590-604), in the year 593, commanded that the baptistery be removed from the monastery of St. Andrew on account of the insolence of the monks. In place of the font he ordered that an altar be erected.[54] Gradually, with the universal establishment of baptismal churches, it was forbidden to any of the monks and regulars to baptize except with the consent of the bishop. The Council of Poitiers (1100) expressly legislated that monks should not presume to baptize.[55]

These baptismal churches had priests permanently assigned to them, and they formed a sort of parish within the cathedral parish. The fundamental right of these priests was to confer baptism on Holy Saturday and on the eve of Pentecost. Martène indicated that for a baptismal church it was necessary to have a deacon along with a priest assigned to it.[56]

As early as the sixth century some councils had spoken of the territory of the baptismal church as a *parochia*.[57] This territory up until the eleventh century was rather extensive and often embraced several villages with their chapels and minor churches. By the time of the Council of Trent the number of churches embracing smaller parochial territory had greatly increased. Thus the baptismal churches were the first foundations of the parochial system.[58]

---

[52] C. 16, C. LVI, q. 1: "Plures baptismales ecclesiae una terminatione esse non possunt, sed una tantummodo cum capellis suis."

[53] Martigny, *Dictionnaire des Antiquités Chrétiennes*, p. 74.

[54] Martène, *De Antiquis Ritibus Ecclesiae*, I, 12.

[55] Canon 10: "Ut clericis regularibus iussu episcopi sui baptizare . . . liceat." Canon 11: "Ut nullus monachorum parochiale ministerium presbyterorum, id est, baptizare . . . praesumat."—Mansi, XX, 1124.

[56] *De Antiquis Ritibus Ecclesiae*, I, 13.

[57] Council of Epaon (506), canon 25—Bruns, II, 183; II Council of Vaison (529), canon 1—Bruns, II, 183.

[58] Kurtscheid, *Historia Iuris Canonici, Historia Institutorum*, I, 278.

CHAPTER III

The Time and the Place of Baptism From the Council of Trent to the Present Code

SECT. I. THE TIME FOR THE ADMINISTRATION OF BAPTISM

As was stated in an earlier chapter, the determination of the particular and only times for the administration of baptism was no longer urged under precept when it was the baptism of infants that became common, and the baptism of adults that became exceptional. From the ninth to the eleventh centuries there was a gradual abolition of the law which determined the exclusive days for baptism.

Schmalzgrueber (1663-1735) stated that the vigils of Easter and Pentecost were no longer observed as the only days on which baptism was administered. Unlike the bishops of the early Church, the bishops in later centuries permitted little by little the administration of baptism to all at any time.[1] As a consequence of this, later legislation in the Church has not treated of any determined time for the reception of baptism, except that it has continued to exhort the administration of the sacrament on the vigils of Easter and Pentecost, when it can be conveniently arranged, in view namely of the liturgical significance of these days.

SECT. II. THE ELEMENT OF TIME IN THE PREPARATION OF THE ADULT FOR BAPTISM

In regard to the time element for the preparation of adults for the reception of baptism, there seems lacking all evidence of any universal legislation on this matter after the catechumenate, in the strict sense, ceased to be practiced by the Church. The Council of Trent (1545-1563) did not treat of this particular matter

[1] *Ius Ecclesiasticum Universum* (5 vols. in 12, Romae, 1843-1845), Lib. III, Tit. 42, n. 10.

in any of its legislation. In 1590 the I Provincial Council of Fermo legislated that adult converts were to be instructed in the doctrines of the Church for a prescribed period of time before baptism was conferred on them.[2] But the Council itself did not state how long that period of time to last.

Alexander VII (1655-1667) warned those whose duty it was to instruct converts that they be mindful of the dangers of profanation which are the result of ignorance. He prescribed that in the future such instructors should not admit anyone to baptism until he had completely put off the old man and put on Christ, by being sufficiently instructed in the faith.[3] Clement IX (1667-1669) extended and amplified the scope of what was demanded by the prescriptions of Alexander VII.[4]

Barbosa (1589-1649) observed that a catechumen should not receive baptism before he had learned the principal articles of faith, such as the Apostles' Creed, the Commandments, the Lord's Prayer, the Passion of Christ and the Future Judgment. In conjunction with this he stated that if a catechumen was specially instructed in these articles of faith for twenty days, he could receive baptism at the end of that period.[5] In commenting on this matter, Schmalzgrueber asserted that if adult converts were sufficiently instructed in their faith, they were obliged under divine command to receive baptism as soon as they could conveniently do so. As a reason for this, he further stated that, since one is obliged to become a member of the Church as soon as possible, he is thereby also obliged to receive baptism as soon as he can do so.[6]

At the beginning of the last century the Sacred Congregation for the Propagation of the Faith stated in a decree for mission territory that the determination of the time and curriculum of

---

[2] Cap. XIII—Mansi, XXXVI B, 901.

[3] Const. *Sacrosancta,* 18 ian. 1858, n. 14—*Fontes,* n. 235.

[4] Const. *In excelsa,* 13 sept. 1669, n. 3—*Fontes,* n. 244.

[5] *Collectanea Decretorum tam Veterum quam Recentiorum in Ius Pontificium Universum* (6 vols. in 3, Lugduni, 1715), Cap. (*Ante Baptismum*), 54, D. IV, *de cons.*

[6] *Op. cit.,* lib. III, tit. 42, n. 10.

the catechumenate should in each case be committed to the prudence and piety of the vicar apostolate.[7]

SECT. III. THE TIME OF BAPTISM IN REGARD TO INFANTS

In its consideration of infant baptism, the Council of Trent did not state exactly or approximately at what time after birth an infant, outside the danger of death, should receive baptism. The Council, however, did condemn those who claimed baptism should be delayed until the age at which Christ received baptism.[8] Moreover, it also condemned those who claimed that inasmuch as children do not have actual faith they should, after having received baptism in their infancy, be rebaptized when they reach the age of reason. The Council also denounced those who teach that it is better to omit the baptism of infants than to baptize them in the faith of the Church.[9]

In a previous article it has been noted that Pope Eugene IV, in the Council of Florence (1439-1445), legislated that infants were to be baptized *quamprimum.*[10] After the time of the Council of Trent, some councils explicitly indicated a specific period of time within which an infant should be baptized. Concerning this matter some councils decreed that the baptism of an infant should not be deferred beyond eight days after birth,[11] while another council prohibited the delay of infant baptism beyond the sixth day after birth.[12]

Several councils restricted even to three days the period of time

---

[7] S. C. de Prop. Fide (C. P. pro Sin.), 20 febr. 1801—*Collectanea S. Congregationis de Propaganda Fide* (2 vols., Romae, 1907), n. 652.

[8] Sess. VII, *de baptismo,* canon 12; Schroeder, *Canons and Decrees of the Council of Trent* (St. Louis: B. Herder Book Co., 1941), p. 54.

[9] Sess. VII, *de baptismo,* canon 13; Schroeder, *op. cit.,* p. 54.

[10] Const. *Cantate Domino,* 4 febr. 1441—*Fontes,* n. 54.

[11] Council of Aix (1585), Tit. VI—Mansi, XXXIV B, 945; Prov. Council of Rouen (1850), Decr. XIII, *de baptismo—Acta et Decreta Sacrorum Conciliorum Recentiorum, Collectio Lacensis* (7 vols., Friburgi Brisgoviae: Herder, 1870-1892), IV, 527 (hereafter cited as *Coll. Lac.*).

[12] I Prov. Council of Quito (1863), Decr. III—Coll. Lac., VI, 402.

within which after birth an infant should receive baptism.[13] In legislating that an infant should be baptized within three days after birth, the Provincial Council of Benevento (1693) made an exception in the case of a child born within two weeks before the vigil of Easter or the vigil of Pentecost. The baptism of all children born within two weeks of these days, unless they were in danger of death, was to be deferred and administered on the vigil of the approaching feast.[14]

From time to time certain councils attached to their decrees a penalty of excommunication for the parents or guardians of a child who neglected to offer their children for baptism within the period of time determined in the decree.[15] Among them the I Council of Milan (1565), presided over by St. Charles Borromeo (1538-1584), decreed that if the parents neglected to bring their children to church for baptism before the ninth day after birth, they would incur the penalty of excommunication.[16]

In 1734 Pope Clement XII (1730-1740) urged preachers to point out to parents their grave duty in conscience to have their children baptized within the designated period of time after birth.[17] Almost a decade later, Pope Benedict XIV (1740-1758) prescribed that the priest who assisted at the marriage ceremony should, with paternal charity, warn the spouses of their obligation to have all children born of their marriage baptized as soon as possible.[18] Regarding the obligation of pastors concerning infant baptism, Schmalzgrueber stated that if parents or tutors neglect their duty to have their children baptized as soon as possible after birth, then their pastor, by reason of his office, should interpose his

---

[13] Prov. Council of Benevento (1693), tit. XXXVI, cap. VIII—*Coll. Lac.*, I, 70; Prov. Council of Avignon (1725), tit. XXV, cap. V—*Coll. Lac.*, I, 523; Prov. Council of Cologne (1860), tit. II, cap. XI—*Coll. Lac.*, V, 348.

[14] Tit. XXXVI, cap. VIII—*Coll. Lac.*, I, 70.

[15] Council of Aix (1585), tit. VI—Mansi, XXXIV B, 945; I Council of Fermo (1590), cap. XIII—Mansi, XXXVI B, 901; Council of Naples (1699), tit. III, cap. II—*Coll. Lac.*, I, 180.

[16] Pars II, tit. II—Mansi, XXXIV A, 15.

[17] Litt. ap. *Compertum,* 24 aug. 1734, dub. IV—*Fontes,* n. 296.

[18] Ep. encycl. *Satis Vobis,* 17 nov. 1741, § 9—*Fontes,* n. 319.

authority in this matter by correcting and admonishing them for their neglect.[19]

Pope Leo XIII (1878-1903) lamented the inveterate abuse of deferring the baptism of children for weeks, months, and sometimes years. He said that nothing was more contrary to ecclesiastical law, since such a practice not only jeopardized the eternal salvation of souls, but also as a consequence of the delay deprived them of the gift of sanctifying grace, which is infused through the sacrament of baptism.[20]

Since in missionary lands priests quite often could not be present in a particular territory for weeks and months, it was generally impossible for Catholics to fulfill the law of the Church by having their children baptized in a short time after birth. As long as the children were not in an immediate danger of death, the parents could not presume to have their children baptized by any of the laity. As a consequence, the Sacred Congregation for the Propagation of the Faith granted permission to catechists in missionary territories to confer private baptism on infants, if a priest was not present in the vicinity within a short time after an infant's birth.

The use of this faculty did not postulate the existence of any urgent necessity or of the danger of death for its lawful exercise. All that was postulated was the absence of the priest from the territory; during his continued absence the administration of private baptism could take the place of the solemn baptism that normally would have been conferred.[21]

At a later time this Congregation, in a letter to the Vicar Apostolic of Corea, gave permission to catechists to confer private baptism on infants ten days after their birth, provided that no missionary had the opportunity of being present in the territory during that time.[22] With reference to the conferring of baptism by

---

[19] *Ius Ecclesiasticum Universum,* lib. III, tit. 42, n. 11.

[20] Ep. *Gratiae,* 22 iul. 1899—Fontes, n. 641.

[21] S. C. de Prop. Fide (C. P. pro Sin.), 21 ian. 1788—*Fontes,* n. 4618. S. C. de Prop. Fide (C. P. pro Sin.-Cochinchin.), 16 ian. 1804—*Fontes,* n. 4677.

[22] S. C. de Prop. Fide, litt. (ad Vic Ap. Coreae), 11 sept. 1841—*Fontes,* n. 4795.

catechists, the Sacred Congregation in 1902 issued a statement reminding missionaries that it was necessary for infants to receive baptism at least within eight days after birth. Furthermore, it stated that it was necessary to eradicate the erroneous opinion of some that the baptism thus given outside a church was only a ceremony and had to be repeated after the advent of the missionary.[23]

SECT. IV. THE TIME AND THE PLACE OF BAPTISM IN CASES OF NECESSITY

In the early Church, as it has been observed in a previous chapter, a number of popes and councils regulated that in cases of necessity baptism could be administered at any time and in any place. None of these decrees or canons made any particular distinctions between solemn and private baptism. Such a distinction came only at a much later date.

In the administration of baptism in the early Church, many ceremonies preceded and followed the essential rite itself of baptism, and often these ceremonies extended over a period of time. By contrast, the Church in later times retained in a shorter form these ancient ceremonies and the accompanying prayers which had given such great solemnity to the sacrament of baptism. It was this shortened form that eventually became constituted as the litany of solemn baptism.[24]

Since in a case of necessity the essential part of baptism could not be delayed through the use of long ceremonies, it is true that even in the early Church these ceremonies must on such an occasion have been dispensed with. The Church designated as a private baptism this administration of the essential part of baptism, when the act of baptizing remained unaccompanied with the usually employed ceremonies. Thus in the course of time there arose the distinction between solemn and private baptism. This distinction was of particular importance in cases of necessity, when only the essential part of the baptismal rite was conferred; but,

---

[23] S. C. de Prop. Fide, instr., 31 iul. 1902—*Fontes,* n. 4940.

[24] Torquebiau, "Baptême en Occident," *Dictionnaire de Droit Canonique,* II, 150.

if the baptized person recovered, the ceremonies had later to be supplied.

In danger of death or in any illness in which it was prudently foreseen that the child of heretics would not live to reach the age of reason, the Sacred Congregation of the Holy Office stated that it was not only licit but also obligatory for missionaries to have such a child baptized without delay. It recommended that, if it was possible, such a child should be baptized in the church, but because of the great probability of opposition on the part of the parents the baptism could be conferred privately at home.[25]

At a later date it was decreed that in the case of infidels who would not permit their children to be taken to the church for baptism, the missionaries were to try to persuade the parents to retract this unreasonable opposition. In the event that they did not succeed in persuading the parents, the extant circumstances were to be construed as creating a case of necessity, and the child could be licitly baptized outside the church, either at home or in a place acceptable to the parents. But in such circumstances the ceremonies of solemn baptism were to be omitted, and the child was later to be brought to the church to have them supplied as soon as possible. If, however, it was foreseen that the parents would remain obstinate, and in the course of time would not give their consent for the child to be taken to the church, then it was licit to use these ceremonies in a private home or some other suitable place.[26] Over a century later the Sacred Congregation of the Holy Office gave the same reply in a similar case and made reference to this very Instruction.[27]

Still later, when there was presented to the Sacred Congregation a case in which the parents who lived at a distance from the church feared that the inclement weather would harm the child, the Congregation urged the missionaries to dissuade the parents from such an unreasonable opinion. If the parents refused to

---

[25] S. C. S. Off. (Siam), 21 ian. 1767—*Fontes,* n. 819.

[26] S. C. de Prop. Fde, instr. (ad Mission. Loanghi), 30 aug. 1775—*Fontes,* n. 4569.

[27] S. C. C. Off., instr. (ad Archiep. Portus Principis), 5 sept. 1877—*Fontes,* n. 1053.

heed the missionaries, the Congregation was ready to consider the situation as equal to a case of necessity, since it was otherwise impossible to procure the baptism of the child while he was under his parents' care. Under such conditions the child was to be given simply a private baptism, and the rites and ceremonies that regularly accompany baptism were to be supplied as soon as possible.[28]

In the case of an adult who when well instructed and disposed was baptized in danger of death, the ceremonies of baptism could later be supplied at home when it was foreseen that most probably before death the person could not be taken to church.[29]

The Sacred Congregation of Rites prescribed that in a case of necessity all the ceremonies which precede baptism should be omitted, and should afterwards be supplied in church when the child regains health.[30] This same legislation concerning private baptism was also included in the canons of several councils during the nineteenth century.[31]

SECT. V. THE CHURCH AS THE PROPER PLACE OF SOLEMN BAPTISM

Art. 1. The Parochial Church

In harmony with the development of parochial rights, the proper place for conferring baptism was no longer limited solely to the cathedral church for all the rural and urban districts of the whole diocese, or even for just the faithful who lived within the boundaries of the city in which the cathedral was situated. As it has been observed in the previous chapter, baptismal churches were erected first in the rural districts, and later in the city areas for the purpose of administering baptism to the faithful who lived

[28] S. C. de Prop. Fide (C. P. pro Sin.), 21 ian. 1789—*Fontes,* n. 4625.

[29] S. C. S. Off. (Tchely Meridio-Oriental.), 10 apr. 1861, n. 2—*Fontes,* n. 965.

[30] S. R. C., *Calaguritana.,* 23 sept. 1820—*Fontes,* n. 5839.

[31] Prov. Council of Avignon (1849), tit. IV, cap. II, *De Baptismo—Coll. Lac.,* IV, 337; Prov. Council of Bourdeaux (1850), tit. III, cap. II—*Coll. Lac.,* IV, 568; Prov. Council of Ravenna (1855), Pars II, cap. II—*Coll. Lac.,* VI, 152; *Acta et Decreta Concilii Plenarii Americae Latinae in Urbe Celebrati Anno Domini MDCCCXCIX* (Romae, 1902), n. 499.

within their district. Gradually as the number of such churches increased, their territorial boundaries grew smaller, until finally most of these churches were recognized as parish churches with full parochial rights.[32]

As the number of these parish churches with baptisteries increased, the fact was more and more acknowledged that in each parish the pastor should baptize his own subjects.[33] But despite this increasing relationship between the proper place of baptism and the parish church, they were not at first recognized as identical. Pignatelli (+ca. 1675) stated that the children of one parish might be baptized in another parish church, since he did not consider the baptismal font as essential to a parish church.[34] Schmalzgrueber, in commenting on the place of baptism, stated that baptism should be conferred in a church in which there is a baptismal font. He made no direct observation concerning the fact whether or not the church should be the parish church.[35]

In 1585 the Council of Aix legislated that baptismal fonts should be erected in all the churches of the province, without making any distinction between parochial and non-parochial churches.[36] Again in a decree of the Sacred Congregation for the Propagation of the Faith, it stated that the sacrament of baptism should be conferred in a church or sacred edifice dedicated to divine worship, but it made no explicit mention of a parish or quasi-parish church or mission church.[37]

According to Fagnanus (1598-1678), however, the proper church for baptism was the parochial church. He stated, without making any complete reference, that the Sacred Congregation

---

[32] Kurtscheid, *Historia Iuris Canonici, Historia Institutorum,* p. 282.

[33] Joseph Waldron, *The Minister of Baptism,* The Catholic University of America Canon Law Studies, n. 170 (Washington, D. C.: The Catholic University of America Press, 1942), p. 48.

[34] *Consultationes Canonicae* (6 vols., Coloniae Allobrogum, 1700), Tome IV, Consultatio III, n. 13.

[35] *Ius Ecclesiasticum Universum,* Lib. III, tit. 42, n. 50.

[36] Tit. VI—Mansi, XXXIV B, 943.

[37] S. C. de Prop. Fide, instr. (ad Mission. Loanghi), 30 aug. 1775—*Fontes,* n. 4569.

of the Council wanted a baptismal font erected in every parish church.[38]

In the past several centuries a number of provincial councils decreed that the parochial church was the proper place for the administration of solemn baptism.[39]

Finally, in 1891, the Sacred Congregation of the Council decreed that in every parochial church, large or small, a baptismal font should be erected.[40] Thus by this decree the Sacred Congregation definitely declared that the administration of solemn baptism was the right and prerogative of the parish church, no matter where it was situated.

The independence of parochial churches in the exercise of baptismal rights is further demonstrated in regard to the blessing of the baptismal font. From an early date the custom existed of blessing baptismal water on Holy Saturday and the Vigil of Pentecost in the cathedral, collegiate and in some special parochial churches. The baptismal water was brought from these churches to the remaining parochial churches. In 1892 the Sacred Congregation of Rites said this custom could no longer be tolerated in the case of parish churches. But in the case of baptismal churches, if there were such, it permitted that they obtain the baptismal water from the cathedral or parochial church.[41] A few years later, this same Congregation explicitly stated that baptismal water should be blessed on Holy Saturday and on the Vigil of Pentecost in all parochial churches and likewise in all other non-parochial churches in which there was lawfully erected a baptismal font.[42]

Even the cathedral church did not possess the right of having

---

[38] *Commentaria in Quinque Libros Decretalium* (3 vols., Venetiis, 1709), Lib. III, tit. *De Decimis*, cap. XXIX, n. 59.

[39] Prov. Council of Naples (1699), tit. III, cap. II—*Coll. Lac.*, I, 180; Prov. Council of Sens (1850), tit. II, cap. II—*Coll. Lac.*, IV, 889; Council of Prague (1860), tit. IV, cap. II—*Coll. Lac.*, V, 490; Prov. Council of Avignon (1849), tit. IV, cap. II—*Coll. Lac.*, IV, 337.

[40] *Acta Sanctae Ledis* (41 vols., Romae, 1865-1903), XXIV (1891-1892), 358. (Hereafter cited *ASS.*)

[41] S. R. C., *Spalaten.*, 7 iun. 1892—*Fontes*, n. 6215.

[42] S. R. C., *Utinen.*, 13 ian. 1899—*Fontes*, n. 6287.

a baptismal font by the mere fact that it was the first church in the diocese. The Sacred Congregation of Rites decreed that a baptismal font should not be erected in a cathedral which had no parish territory attached to it.[43]

Art. 2. The Non-Parochial Church

In order to receive baptism in a parish church other than that within the boundaries of which the child was born, the Council of Toulouse (1850) decreed that the permission of the bishop or of the pastor of the child had to be obtained.[44] The Provincial Council of Auch (1851) went still further by prohibiting priests under the penalty of suspension to baptize anyone outside his parish church, except in a case of danger of death or with the permission of the ordinary.[45] As a source of convenience to people who lived at a long distance from the parish church, the Provincial Council of Urbino (1859) decreed that with the permission of the bishop and without prejudice to parochial rights a baptismal font might be erected within a church other than the parochial church.[46]

When a new parish was created through the division of a large parish, it was permitted in many cases under the old law to have the baptismal right reserved exclusively to the original parish. As a consequence, the new parish could not erect a baptismal font, unless it was given the right to do so.[47] But in some cases a church other than the parochial church was permitted to have cumulative rights with one or several parish churches in regard to the administration of baptism. St. Peter's at Rome was recognized as a proper place of baptism for all the people living in the city, so that it had along with all the parish churches of Rome the cumulative right of conferring baptism.[48]

---

[43] S. R. C., Oveten., 31 aug. 1872—*Fontes,* n. 6046.

[44] Tit. III, cap. I, n. LXI—*Coll. Lac.*, IV, 1052.

[45] Tit. III, cap. I—*Coll. Lac.,* IV, 1184.

[46] Pars. I, tit. IV, cap. XI—*Coll. Lac.,* VI, 11.

[47] Woywod, *A Practical Commentary on the Code of Canon Law* (10. ed., 2 vols., New York: Wagner, 1946), I, 355.

[48] S. C. C., *Romana,* 15 maii 1700—*Analecta Iuris Pontificii,* VIII (1866), 1594.

In order that a church could claim a cumulative right over the faithful of another parish, it was necessary to show that this right was long established through custom or by lawful authority. In cases in which the long establishment of such a right could not be proved, the church could no longer administer baptism to those outside its parish territory. Thus the Sacred Congregation of the Council refused to the pastor of the Cathedral of Fabriano the cumulative right of baptizing the children of other parishes, since this right could not be satisfactorily established.[49]

The II Plenary Council of Baltimore (1866) directed that the sacrament of baptism should never be administered outside a church except in danger of death. To those parents who lived in rural districts, villages, or small towns where there was no church, it granted permission to bring their children to the nearest church in which baptism was usually conferred.[50]

SCHOLION. THE BAPTISMAL FONT

St. Charles Borromeo (1538-1584) in the IV Provincial Council of Milan (1576) decreed certain norms that were to be followed in regard to the custody of baptismal fonts. In these norms, which have served as the basis of later legislation concerning baptismal fonts, it was stated that a baptismal font was to be made of marble or solid stone. Moreover, every baptistery was to be protected by means of at least a wooden grating, and the baptismal font was to be located at the entrance of the church, unless in some cases the bishop for a good reason permitted that it could be placed in another part of the church. For the future it was decreed that every bishop should see to it that a chapel in which

---

[49] *Analecta Iuris Pontificii,* VIII (1866), 1595; *Thesaurus Resolutionum S. C. Concilii ab anno 1718* (167 vols., Urbini, 1718-1741; Romae, 1741-1908), V, 277.

[50] *Concilii Plenarii Baltimorensis II, in Ecclesia Metropolitana Baltimorensi, a die VII ad diem XXI Octobris A. D. MDCCCLXVI Habiti et a Sede Apostolica Recogniti Acta et Decreta* (Baltimorae: Joannes Murphy, 1868), n. 237.

the baptismal font was located should be built in the parish churches, especially in the more distinguished churches.[51]

Similar legislation was made in the Council of Aix (1585),[52] the I Council of Fermo (1590),[53] the I Provincial Council of Westminster (1852),[54] the Provincial Council of Cashel (1853),[55] and the Provincial Council of Ravenna (1856).[56]

SECT. VI. SOLEMN BAPTISM IN PRIVATE HOMES

Art. 1. Upon Legitimate Request

In 1751 Pope Benedict XIV (1740-1758) reiterated the law established by Pope Clement V, in the Council of Vienne (1311), determining the occasions on which the sacrament of baptism with all the ceremonies and rites could be lawfully conferred at home.[57] In particular, Pope Benedict made mention of the fact that the administration of solemn baptism to the children of kings and supreme rulers in their own homes was in harmony with the law.[58] A few years later the Sacred Congregation of the Holy Office also made reference to the same decree of Pope Clement concerning the solemn baptism of the children of supreme temporal rulers. It verified the fact that such children could be baptized at home.[59]

In regard to this point, Zitelli (+1887) stated that solemn baptism could lawfully be administered at home not only to the children of rulers, but also, when custom so allowed it, to the children of nobles, provided that it was conferred in the oratories of their houses.[60] Schmalzgrueber, in mentioning the decree of Pope

---

[51] Pars II, cap. 2—Hardouin, *Acta Conciliorum et Epistolae Decretales ac Constitutiones Summorum Pontificum* (12 vols., Parisiis, 1715), X, 839.

[52] Tit. VI—Mansi, XXXIV B, 945.

[53] Cap. XIII—Mansi, XXXVI B, 901.

[54] Decr. XVI—*Coll. Lac.,* III, 928.

[55] Decr. III, tit. III—*Coll. Lac.,* 833.

[56] Pars II, cap. II—*Coll. Lac.,* VI, 152.

[57] C. un., *de baptismo et eius effectu,* III, 15, in Clem.

[58] Ep. encycl. *Magno cum,* 2 iun. 1751—*Fontes,* n. 413.

[59] S. C. S. Off. instr. (ad Praef. Mission. Tripol.), mense ian. 1763—*Fontes,* n. 812.

[60] *Apparatus Iuris Ecclesiastici* (Romae, 1886), p. 308.

Clement, claimed that the privilege could be extended also to illustrious and influential persons, under the proviso that this was the custom in the place where these persons lived.[61]

In considering this point, Caponi, a canonical writer of the seventeenth century, observed that the children of rulers and kings should be baptized in a chapel or hall of their residence. Moreover, he added that if any pastor without special permission baptized an infant in a private chamber or in the bedroom of the ruler's house he had to abstain from the exercise of his office for six months. He believed that the decree of Pope Clement, in addition to the children of rulers, also included the children of the wealthy. He stated that under the name of children the grandchildren of rulers were also comprehended. Both the children and the grandchildren, however, had to be of legitimate status before the decree became applicable in their favor.[62] Lancelotti (1522-1590) understood the decree to embrace not only the children of rulers but also the children of those who had notable power or influence. He observed, however, that the children of tyrants did not enjoy this privilege.[63]

In the legislation of the Council of Aix (1585) it was decreed that a pastor or any other priest should not administer solemn baptism at home to the children of important people, except in a case of necessity, for otherwise a priest who administered baptism to the children of such people would incur an excommunication. This decree of the Provincial Council was indeed not in harmony with the opinion of the authors. It must be remembered, however, that these canonists considered the privilege of the decree of Pope Clement to be extended to such people only when local custom allowed it.[64]

Art. 2. With the Permission of the Ordinary

After the Council of Trent the legislation concerning the proper place of baptism prohibited the administration of solemn baptism

[61] *Ius Ecclesiasticum Universum,* lib. III, tit. 42, n. 50.

[62] *Institutiones Canonicae* (2. ed., 2 vols. in 1, Coloniae Allobrogum, 1734), I, 243.

[63] *Institutiones Iuris Canonici* (Venetiis, 1704), lib. III, tit. 3, n. 19.

[64] Tit. VI—Mansi, XXXIV B, 945.

at home, except under the conditions laid down in the decree of Pope Clement V. The Sacred Congregation of the Council in 1635 stated that it disapproved of the custom of baptizing children in their homes as soon as they were born. In conjunction with this, it is urged that care be taken to observe the decree of Pope Clement.[65]

Over a century later the Sacred Congregation of the Holy Office permitted missionaries, in their prudent judgment, to confer solemn baptism at home on children born of Catholic parents if they lived at such a distance from the mission church that they could not bring their children to the baptismal font without a morally certain danger of great inconvenience and even of the death of the child.[66] In like manner the Sacred Congregation of Rites within the past century allowed missionaries to confer baptism with all the ceremonies in private homes in those mission territories where the Catholic people lived so far from the church that they could not bring their children to the church without some danger.[67]

By contrast, the Sacred Congregation of Rites, in a response not intended for mission territory, gave a stricter answer when it was asked whether, with the testimony of a doctor concerning the danger of taking a child to church for baptism, it could be permitted by the bishop to have such a child baptized at home with all the ceremonies. In its reply it said that care must be taken prudently and cautiously to remove this abuse, and to have the child baptized at church according to the common practice.[68]

As a consequence of these decrees, people of missionary territory who lived at a far distance from the church enjoyed the favor of having their children baptized at home, when there was present a probable danger or some grave inconvenience. But in regard to the faithful of other localities, such a cause as that of inconvenience was not deemed sufficient to allow them to have their children baptized at home.

---

[65] S. C. C., *Belgii,* 16 iun. 1635—*Fontes,* n. 2576.

[66] S. C. S. Off., instr. (ad Praef. Mission. Tripol.), mense ian. 1763—*Fontes,* n. 812.

[67] S. R. C., *Vicariatus Apostolici de Dania,* 10 febr. 1871—*Fontes,* n. 6035.

[68] S. R. C., *Asculana in Piceno,* 27 apr. 1877—*Fontes,* n. 6097.

Several councils, however, legislated that baptism with all the ceremonies could be conferred in private homes, if there was a grave cause, and if permission was obtained from the ordinary.[69]

In order to have a grave cause present it was not necessary that a probable danger exist, for any prudent fear, presumption, or conjecture that a child might die without baptism or contract a disease, if he were brought to church, sufficed to permit solemn baptism at home.[70] Moreover, it was permitted to baptize an infant at home with all the baptismal ceremonies, if the child could not be publicly baptized in church without infamy to the mother. Again, if a child had already been baptized in church, but afterwards, for some reason, it became necessary to repeat the sacrament conditionally, then in such a case baptism could be administered at home.[71]

If the locality of the parents or guardian whose duty it was to bring the child to church for baptism was blockaded or besieged, or if they had public enemies along the road between their home and the church, then Giraldi (1692-1775) considered these factors as grave causes that required that such a child be baptized at home.[72]

When a grave or reasonable cause did not exist, the administration of baptism at home could not indeed be allowed. Thus the Council of Prague condemned the abuse of administering baptism to infants in their homes in view simply of the entreaties of their parents. It reminded pastors that they were bound in conscience to remove such an abuse, as soon as possible, from places where it existed.[73] When the United States was still considered a mission territory, the II Plenary Council of Baltimore (1866) left it to the prudence and conscience of the missionaries to baptize

---

[69] Roman Council (1725), tit. XXVI, cap. III—*Coll. Lac.*, I, 387; Prov. Council of Cologne (1860), tit. II, cap. XI—*Coll. Lac.*, V, 348; *Acta et Decreta Concilii Plenarii Americae Latinae in Urbe Celebrati Anno Domini MDCCCXCIX*, n. 499.

[70] Schmalzgrueber, *Ius Ecclesiasticum Universum*, lib. III, tit. 42, n. 50.

[71] Zitelli, *Apparatus Iuris Ecclesiastici*, p. 308.

[72] *Expositio Iuris Pontificii iuxta Recentiorem Ecclesiae Disciplinam*, lib. III, pars I, tit. XLII, sect. DCXVIII.

[73] Council of Prague (1860), tit. IV, cap. II—*Coll. Lac.*, 490.

children in their homes with all the ceremonies of the Church, if because of inclement weather, extreme difficulty of traveling, the need of the parents, or other grave causes the child could not be taken to the church.[74]

If in a certain territory or area there was no church or oratory in which the public could attend divine services, then it was the duty of the priest to administer solemn baptism to children in their homes.[75]

---

[74] *Concilii Plenarii Baltimorensis II, in Ecclesia Metropolitana Baltimorensi, a die VII ad diem XXI Octobris, A.D. MDCCCLXVI Habiti, et a Sede Apostolica Recogniti Acta et Decreta*, n. 237.

[75] Zitelli, *Apparatus Iuris Ecclesiastici*, p. 308.

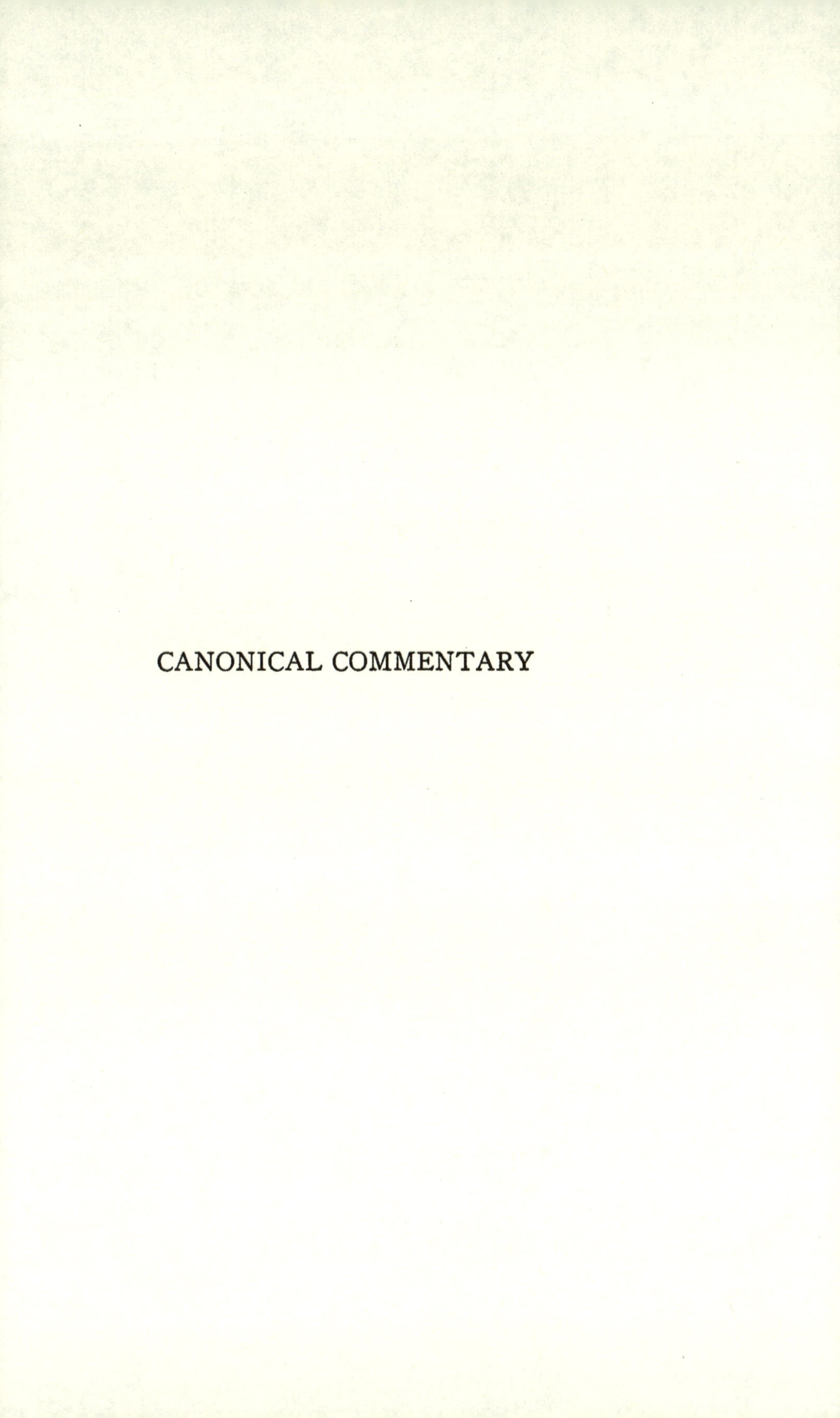

CANONICAL COMMENTARY

CHAPTER IV

The Element of Time in Regard to Baptism

Sect. I. The Proper Time for the Administration of Baptism

Art. 1. The Days for the Administration of Baptism

In legislating concerning the proper days for the administration of solemn baptism, the Code does not oblige its subjects to a strict observance. Rather the Code makes a special recommendation in this matter, from which one may rightfully abstract whenever there exists a sufficient cause for warranting the selection of a day differing from those stated in the law. As a consequence the Code, in determining the time proper for solemn baptism, in no manner intends to affect the licitness of the administration of solemn baptism.

In regard to infants and those who have not attained the use of reason,[1] the ecclesiastical law permits that they may receive solemn baptism on any day in the year.[2] Thus the sacrament of baptism may be solemnly administered to this group, who are not considered subjects of ecclesiastical law,[3] on any Sunday or weekday during the year, on a feast day or a ferial day, and even on Good Friday.[4]

Solemn baptism may be administered to infants, and to those who are devoid of the use of reason, even on a day during a period of time when a general local interdict is placed upon a diocese or parish in which the child is to be baptized.[5] The general local interdict which may affect an entire parish can be imposed by the ordinary in whose diocese the parish is situated. Likewise the general local interdict may affect even an entire diocese, but

---

[1] Canon 745, § 2, 1°.

[2] Canon 772.

[3] Canon 12.

[4] Fanfani, *De Iure Parochorum* (Romae: Marietti, 1924), p. 217.

[5] Canon 2269, § 1.

the issuing of such an interdict is not within the power of the ordinary. It can be imposed only by the Apostolic See.[6] Unless it is expressly stated otherwise in the decree of the interdict, solemn baptism may be administered in the cathedral and in parish churches during the time of such a general local interdict.[7] During the time of such an interdict it is not required that a case of necessity exist before solemn baptism can be administered, but rather the sacrament can be conferred on any infant who is offered for baptism, whether necessity urges or not, and provided all other required conditions are fulfilled.[8]

Likewise the Code allows the administration of solemn baptism to adults on any day of the year, but in its legislation it shows special preference for two particular days in the year, the vigils of Easter and of Pentecost.[9] By its use of the word *decet* the Code gives sufficient indication that ecclesiastical law does not strictly bind all adult converts to be baptized on only these days. Rather, these days are recommended as the more fitting days in the ecclesiastical calendar on which solemn baptism may be conferred. But the Code makes every allowance for the choice of another day, when a sufficient cause is present by including in its legislation the words *si fieri commode queat.*

The term *adult* points to those who have the use of reason. Thus it embraces those who can seek baptism of their own free will.[10] It is opposed to the term *infans,* or *parvulus,* which points to persons who have not yet attained the use of reason. A person who

---

[6] Conran, *The Interdict,* The Catholic University of America Canon Law Studies, n. 56 (Washington, D. C.: The Catholic University of America, 1930), p. 59.

[7] Canon 2271, 2°; Fanfani, *De Iure Parochorum,* p. 217; Blat, *Commentarium Textus Codicis Iuris Canonici* (5 vols. in 6, Romae: ex Typographia Pontificia in Instituto Pii IX, 1919-1927), Lib. III, Pars I, n. 6 (hereafter cited *Commentarium*).

[8] Blat, *loc. cit.*

[9] Canon 772; *Rituale Romanum Pauli V Pontificis Maximi iussu editum aliorumque Pontificum cura recognitum atque auctoritate SSmi D. N. Pii Papae XI ad normam Codicis Iuris Canonici Accommodatum* (Editio iuxta Typicam Vaticanam, Mechliniae: Typis H. Dessain, 1926), tit. II, cap. 3, n. 3.

[10] Canon 745, § 2, 2°.

has been insane from infancy is equivalently regarded as an *infans* or a *parvulus*. Before the age of seven a person is presumed not to have the use of reason.[11] As a consequence, the positive aspect of this presumption implies that after the seventh year of age a person is considered to have attained the use of reason, and is thus regarded as an adult in respect to the reception of baptism. This presumption, however, is a *presumptio iuris*,[12] which will admit direct or indirect proof to the contrary.[13] In the absence of contrary proof, a minor who has completed his seventh year of age is considered an adult subject for the reception of baptism. Such a person has a right to receive baptism when he comprehends the meaning and purpose of baptism, and when he conscientiously expresses a wish to receive it, even though his parents object.[14] In a matter of such great importance as baptism, which involves the soul's eternal salvation, the law exempts minors from the paternal power.[15]

In its law the Church sets aside these days as preferable for adults, in distinction to infants, because the danger of death is a much more serious threat to infants than to adults. If in the case of infants baptism were delayed for a long time until the vigils of Easter or Pentecost, in many cases they would be exposed to the great danger of dying without baptism. Infants cannot receive baptism of desire, while adults may receive either of three kinds of baptism, namely of water, of desire, and of blood.[16] In the case of an adult who is in a sudden danger of death and for some reason cannot receive baptism of water, then if he has all the necessary dispositions for baptism of water with an act of perfect contrition he can receive baptism of desire. An infant, however, in similar circumstances would be incapable of baptism of desire. Consequently, the Church wishes to place no restrict-

---

[11] Canon 80, § 3.

[12] Canon 1825, § 2.

[13] Canon 1826.

[14] Woywod, *A Practical Commentary on the Code of Canon Law*, I, n. 638.

[15] Cf. canon 89.

[16] Cappello, *Tractatus Canonico-Moralis de Sacramentis* (5 vols., Vol. I, 5. ed., Romae: Marietti, 1947), I, 94 (hereafter cited *De Sacramentis*).

tions on the days proper for the reception of baptism by infants.[17]

In recommending the vigils of Easter and Pentecost as the proper days for the reception of baptism by adults, the Church has in mind the practice of the early Church, in which baptism of adults was absolutely restricted to the Easter and Pentecostal seasons, and later only to the vigils of Easter and Pentecost. Necessity alone allowed a departure from the administration of baptism on these days to both infants and adults. Moreover, the Church also recognizes the deep significance between the mysteries of the Resurrection and Pentecost and the sacrament of baptism.[18] St. Thomas stated that the faithful are baptized on the vigils of Easter and Pentecost, because baptism has its efficacy from the passion of Christ and from the Holy Spirit.[19]

In compliance, therefore, with the law of the Church, adults who have the necessary dispositions, and who have received and completed their instructions before the Easter season, should be asked to wait for the reception of solemn baptism on Holy Saturday. If they have not completed their instructions before Holy Saturday, but only before the vigil of Pentecost, then they should receive solemn baptism on that day. It is not required that their course of instruction be completed immediately before the commencement of the Easter or Pentecostal seasons in order to be baptized on these vigils. Rather, those who have completed their instructions a few weeks or several days before one of these vigils should wait for the reception of baptism on that particular day. But if an adult presents himself for instructions only after Pentecost, and has completed his instructions a few months before Holy Saturday of the following year, it would be a hardship for him to defer baptism to that day. In that case he should be baptized as soon as he has completed his instructions, without being made to wait for the recurrence of these vigils. It may happen, however, by way of exception, as it does in mission coun-

---

[17] Fanfani, *De Iure Parochorum,* p. 217.

[18] Blat, *Commentarium,* Lib. III, Pars I, n. 61; Augustine, *A Commentary on the New Code of Canon Law* (8 vols., Vol. IV, 6. ed., St. Louis: B. Herder Book Co., 1931), IV, 87.

[19] *Summa Theologica,* Pars III, q. LXVI, art. X, ad 1.

tries, that this preparation for baptism will last for a long period of several months, extending from a time shortly after Pentecost to almost the commencement of the Easter season. Again, often enough an adult will not have a good reason to refuse the reception of baptism on the vigils of Easter and Pentecost, but one can well admit that he may feel some embarrassment in receiving the sacrament publicly during the services of Holy Saturday in a parish church.[20] In such a case it would seem better to administer solemn baptism later that day, when the ceremony would be less public and more convenient for him.

Since the Code imposes no obligation, its recommendation need not be strictly observed, and any reasonable cause will justify the conferring of solemn baptism on any other day than the vigils of Easter and Pentecost.

Art. 2. The Time of Day for the Administration of Solemn Baptism

The Code neither explicitly nor implicitly legislates or recommends at what particular hour or part of the day infants are to receive solemn baptism. Fanfani considers it unfitting for infants to be baptized solemnly at night, unless a just cause demands otherwise.[21] Such a cause would exist in the case of the baptism of an illegitimate child. In this case Cappello is of the opinion that the child should be baptized in the early morning or late in the evening with the exclusion of all public solemnity.[22] In the absence of any positive legislation to the contrary in the Code, any just cause will warrant and render fitting the conferring of solemn baptism to infants even at night.

In regard to adults, the Code does not state explicitly at what time of day they should receive baptism, but it does by way of implication legislate that they should be baptized in the morning. The Code prescribes that an adult should assist immediately after

---

[20] De Clercq, *Traité de Droit Canonique* (Publié sous la direction de Raoul Naz, 4 vols., Vol. 2, *Des Sacrements,* Paris: Letouzey et Ané, 1948), II, n. 55.

[21] *De Iure Parochorum,* n. 240.

[22] *De Sacramentis,* I, n. 181.

his baptism at the Holy Sacrifice of the Mass and receive Holy Communion.[23] Since Mass must be offered in the morning,[24] and since the convert is to assist at Mass and receive Holy Communion immediately after his baptism, the Code implicitly legislates that an adult should be baptized in the morning. In addition, the *Roman Ritual,* in conjunction with its statement in canon 753, § 2, explicitly states that the baptism of an adult is to be conferred before noon, unless a reasonable cause excuses.[25] From this statement Augustine (1872-1943) also drew his conclusion that an adult should be baptized in the morning, when this could be conveniently arranged.[26]

Does the Code impose a strict obligation for adults to receive baptism only in the morning? From the words, *nisi graves urgentesque causae obsint,* such would seem to be the case, especially if the word *statim* were to be interpreted according to its proper significance as it is in the text of the canon.[27] Both Cappello[28] and Fanfani[29] consider these precepts to be of grave obligation by reason of the fact that only a grave and urgent cause will excuse an adult from assisting at Mass and receiving Holy Communion immediately after his baptism. Vermeersch (1858-1936) did not attach a strict interpretation to the word *statim,* and therefore did not regard these precepts as involving a grave obligation.[30] Rather, he stated that an urgent excuse is not required for an adult to defer his fulfillment of these precepts, as long as this deferment is not for a long period of time. He interpreted *statim* as allowing for an interval of two or three days. Thus he concluded that the practice of baptizing adults in the evening, and of having

---

[23] Canon 753, § 2.

[24] Canon 821, § 1.

[25] Tit. 2, cap. 3, n. 7, 8: "Quare non post epulas, aut prandia, sed ante meridiem."

[26] *A Commentary on the New Code of Canon Law,* IV, 61.

[27] Canon 18.

[28] *De Sacramentis,* I, 154.

[29] *De Iure Parochorum,* n. 236.

[30] Vermeersch-Creusen, *Epitome Iuris Canonici* (3 vols., Vol. I, 6. ed., 1937; Vol. II, 5. ed., 1934; Vol. III, 5. ed., 1936, Mechliniae-Romae: H. Dessain), II, n. 39.

them assist at Mass and receive Holy Communion on the following day, is perfectly lawful. Augustine likewise was of the opinion that a grave obligation was not discernible in the law of the Code, for he stated that, although the baptism of adults should be conferred in the morning, yet the time of the baptism can be regulated according to the convenience of the subject who is to receive the sacrament.[31] Augustine drew his conclusion from the words of the *Roman Ritual, "si hora congruens fuerit, celebratur Missa, cui neophyti intersunt."*[32] He further added that custom, wherever it so exists, may permit a person to deviate from the obligation of immediate assistance at Mass and reception of Holy Communion.[33]

Other authors are also of the opinion that these precepts are not of strict obligation, and that the doctrine of Vermeersch may be followed in practice because of its extrinsic probability.[34]

De Clercq states that a reasonable cause will permit the deferring of assistance at Mass and the reception of Holy Communion to one or several days, either to the following day, if the adult was baptized in the afternoon, or to the following Sunday, when the baptized adult must attend Mass.[35] It may happen in a particular case that an adult will be baptized in the morning, but will not be able to assist at Mass and receive Holy Communion immediately after baptism, either because of the person's illness and lack of a dispensation from the Eucharistic fast,[36] or because of the inconvenience of delaying the celebration of Mass until the time of the morning when baptism is administered to adults.

In any case the law is not absolutely clear concerning the proper interpretation of the term *statim,* and there are probable opinions on both sides of the question. Since the law, therefore, is doubtful,

---

[31] *A Commentary on the Code of Canon Law,* IV, 61.

[32] Tit. II, cap. IV, n. 51.

[33] *Op. cit.,* IV, p. 61, footnote 52.

[34] Coronata, *Institutiones Iuris Canonici, De Sacramentis Tractatus Canonicus* (3 vols., Taurini: Marietti, 1943-1946), I, n. 134 (hereafter cited *De Sacramentis*); Ayrinhac, *Legislation on the Sacraments in the New Code of Canon Law* (New York: Longmans, Green and Co., 1928), I, n. 34 (hereafter cited as *Legislation on the Sacraments*).

[35] *Traité de Droit Canonique,* II, n. 30.

[36] De Clercq, *loc. cit.*

it cannot be considered to have a binding force.[37] Thus there seems to be no solid ground for objection to the practice of baptizing an adult either in the afternoon or in the evening, as it is usually done in the United States, and of permitting the baptized adult to go to Mass and receive Holy Communion at his convenience either the next day or a few days later.[38]

In conjunction with the precept urging the immediate assistance at Mass and the reception of Holy Communion consequent to the reception of baptism by an adult, there arises the question of the Eucharistic fast. Does the salt given to the adult during the ceremonies of baptism break the fast required by ecclesiastical law for the reception of Holy Communion? In the first place the Code does consider it fitting that the minister and the adults who are to receive baptism, and who are in good health, observe the fast.[39] By the use of the word *decet* the Code apparently imposes no strict obligation, but merely makes a suggestion that is in accord with the ancient discipline of the Church, which required adults to be baptized on the vigils of Easter or Pentecost. These days were observed as days of strict fast in the early Church.[40] It is not the Eucharistic fast, but a baptismal fast, that the Code considers as a fitting preparation for the reception of the sacrament when it is conferred not only in the morning, but at any other time of day, as may occur in an exceptional case for a grave cause or for reasons that are in conformity with the opinion of Vermeersch and other authors.

Strictly regarded, the swallowing of the blessed salt does break the natural fast, for moralists agree that the smallest quantity of food or drink taken before Holy Communion does not allow the reception of Holy Communion, even when the food or drink is taken accidentally.[41] But in accordance with a principle recog-

---

[37] Canon 15.

[38] Woywod, *A Practical Commentary on the Code of Canon Law,* I, n. 646.

[39] Canon 753, § 1.

[40] Woywod, *A Practical Commentary on the Code of Canon Law,* I, n. 646; De Clercq, *Traité de Droit Canonique,* II, n. 30.

[41] Noldin-Schmitt, *Summa Theologiae Moralis* (26. ed., 3 vols., Ratisbonae: Fridericus Pustet, 1940), III, n. 148.

nized by moralists, the law that calls for fasting should not interfere with any of the rites prescribed by the Church.[42] This was made clear in a decree of the Sacred Congregation of the Propagation of the Faith which ordained that the baptized adult not only could but also should receive Holy Communion, "even though the fast seems to be broken."[43] The Congregation used the word *videatur,* and thus implied that the breaking of the fast is not real but apparent. Moreover, the law on the Eucharistic fast is only ecclesiastical in its origin, and an adult before his baptism is not bound by ecclesiastical laws.[44] By baptism an adult does become a subject of ecclesiastical law, and consequently he is from that time on bound to observe the Eucharistic fast. But the Church, by its request that an adult assist at Mass and receive Holy Communion immediately after baptism, implicitly dispenses the recently baptized subject from the Eucharistic fast. Accordingly, he may assist at Mass and receive Holy Communion despite the fact that he has broken his fast.

In conclusion, since there may exist many reasons which would make it very inconvenient or would even prevent an adult from being baptized in the morning and from immediately attending Mass and receiving Holy Communion, he may receive the sacrament in the afternoon or evening, and fulfill these two precepts of the following morning or even within several days of the reception of baptism.

SECT. II. THE ELEMENT OF TIME IN THE PREPARATION OF ADULTS FOR BAPTISM

Art. 1. Adults Outside the Danger of Death

Those adults who are not members of the Catholic Church, and who at some time during their life receive the gift of faith in recognizing the fact that the Catholic Church is the true and only

---

[42] "Salt swallowed does not break the fast."—*The Ecclesiastical Review* (hereafter referred to as *ER*), LVIII (1918), 322.

[43] S. C. de Prop. Fide (ad Vic. Ap. Tunk. Orient.), 16 febr. 1806—*Collectanea S. Congregationis de Propaganda Fide,* n. 687.

[44] Canon 12.

Church founded by Jesus Christ have a grave obligation to enter the Church. For everyone is bound to enter the visible Church, when he recognizes its obligatory character. Since he cannot enter the Church except through baptism, which is the door to the Church, he is held to receive this sacrament as soon as it can be conveniently conferred on him.[45] Noldin (1838-1922) stated that an adult who is cognizant of his obligation to enter the Church by the reception of baptism must at least seek admittance into the catechumenate as soon as it is conveniently possible to him.[46] By the catechumenate he understood the period of preparation before baptism, in which the convert is adequately instructed in Christian doctrine and morals. The ecclesiastical law extends certain privileges to those who are in the catechumenate.[47] In particular, it extends the right of Christian burial[48] to catechumens who during the period of instructions and preparation die without baptism through no fault of their own.[49]

The gravity of the obligation on the part of an adult to receive baptism *quamprimum* is somewhat controverted. In the danger of death no delay in this regard can be tolerated, once an adult recognizes his obligation to enter the Church. But aside from this circumstance, St. Thomas did not consider a delay grave on the part of an adult, unless this deferral was induced by a contempt for baptism or by some other great evil.[50] Suarez (1548-1617), however, considered the reception of baptism *quamprimum* by an adult to be of grave obligation.[51] Only in the case of a moral impossibility did he admit an excuse for the procrastination of baptism over a long period of time. It is agreed upon, however, that the obligation to receive baptism within a certain period of time cannot be determined from the divine law. Since unbaptized

---

[45] Genicot, *Institutiones Theologiae Moralis* (2 vols., Lovanii: Typis et Sumptibus Polleunis et Ceuterick, 1897), II, n. 149; Cappello, *De Sacramentis,* I, n. 148.

[46] *Summa Theologiae Moralis,* III, n. 73.

[47] Canons 1149, 1152.

[48] Canon 1204.

[49] Canon 1239, § 2.

[50] *Summa Theologica,* Supplementum, q. VI, a. 5.

[51] *De Sacramentis,* Pars I, Disp. 31, sect. 11—*Opera Omnia,* XX, 593.

adults, however, are not the subjects of ecclesiastical jurisdiction,[52] the Church certainly does not have the power to determine the time within which they are to receive baptism after the recognition of the serious obligation to be baptized. Although the obligation to receive baptism within a definite period of time cannot be determined from the divine law, nevertheless, because baptism is absolutely necessary for salvation, this same law should operate to require an adult, who is cognizant of his obligation to be baptized, to receive the sacrament as soon as it is convenient to him.[53]

After an adult signifies his intention to receive baptism, he must be instructed in the doctrines of the faith before the actual reception of the sacrament, in order that he may have the necessary dispositions and preparation, which are required by the nature of the sacrament and the law of the Church.[54] Consequently, although an adult should receive baptism as soon as possible, the conferring of the sacrament must be deferred until the time when he has been sufficiently exercised and tested in the things which pertain to a Christian life.[55] Just how long this period of preparation and instruction will last depends, to a large extent, on the prudent judgment of the pastor or priest who will impart these instructions.[56]

In two cases it is proper to dispense with the deferral of baptism for the purpose of instructions and the acquisition of the necessary dispensations. There should be no delay in administering the sacrament when the adult is already very well instructed in the doctrines of the faith, and thus is found ready for baptism. Likewise baptism can be conferred almost immediately, that is after a few instructions, when the adult who seeks it is either old

[52] Canon 12.

[53] Genicot, *Institutiones Theologiae Moralis,* II, n. 149; Noldin-Schmitt, *Summa Theologiae Moralis,* III, n. 73; Coronata, *De Sacramentis,* I, n. 132.

[54] Warnz-Vidal, *Ius Canonicum* (7 vols. in 8, Romae: Universitas Gregoriana, 1923-1938), Tom. IV, Vol. I, nn. 40-41.

[55] Merkelbach, *Summa Theologiae Moralis* (ed. alt., 3 vols., Parisiis: Desclée, de Brouwer et Cie, 1939), III, n. 143.

[56] Sabetti-Barrett, *Compendium Theologiae Moralis* (27. ed., New York: Frederick Pustet Co., Inc., 1919), p. 584.

or quite ill.[57] On the other hand, the reception of baptism can be deferred for a long time when the adult, who otherwise wishes to receive the sacrament, fears grave oppression, either of mind or of body, or some other outrageous evil. Such would be the case when a minor would be dismissed from his father's home and reduced to a state of misery. In this case the convert would receive baptism of desire, if death should overtake him while in such circumstances.[58]

The Code in no way determines the length of time to be devoted to the instruction of an adult for baptism. Thus the duration and the nature of the instructions must be arranged according to age, intellectual capacity and circumstances. In 1883 the Sacred Congregation for the Propagation of the Faith, in an instruction to a Vicar Apostolic in China, declared that the Vicar Apostolic was to determine, in his prudent judgment, the duration of the instructions imparted to adult candidates for baptism.[59] But in a later instruction it urged that these were not to be prolonged over an extended period in the case of old people, of the infirm, of those who showed extraordinary signs of conversion and who gave an outstanding example of fortitude in the time of persecution.[60] Moreover, the Holy Office also asserted that the period of the catechumenate had to be arranged according to the ability of the convert to assimilate the necessary truths.[61] Lehmkuhl (1834-1918) did not consider it of grave obligation for an adult to receive baptism immediately after he has completed the required instructions. In his opinion a delay of one or two months after the final instruction can be tolerated, but inasmuch as there is involved the possible danger of relapse, he urged that the cate-

---

[57] Sabetti-Barrett, *Compendium Theologiae Moralis,* p. 584; De Clercq, *Traité de Droit Canonique,* II, n. 28.

[58] Prümmer, *Manuale Theologiae Moralis* 2. et 3. ed., 3 vols., Friburgi Brisgoviae, 1923), III, n. 134.

[59] S. C. de Prop. Fide (C. P. pro Sin.), 20 febr. 1801—*Collectanea S. Congregationis de Propaganda Fide,* n. 652.

[60] S. C. de Prop. Fide, instr. (ad Vic. Ap. Sin.), 18 oct. 1883—*Fontes,* n. 4903.

[61] S. C. S. Off. (Sutchuen.), 28 sept. 1724—*Fontes,* n. 783; S. C. S. Off. (Quebec), 10 maii 1703, ad 2—*Fontes,* n. 765.

chumenate be terminated with the satisfactory completion of these instructions.[62]

For those who have just attained the use of reason, which is normally the case at the age of seven,[63] and who are thus considered adults for the reception of baptism,[64] the period of time devoted to instruction before the administration of the sacrament should be somewhat shortened, if it is certain that they will pursue a course of religious instructions for several years.[65] But if a minor who wishes to be baptized and embrace the Church seeks to do so against the will of those who have authority over him, the ordinary must always be consulted in such cases.[66] There is no obligation to delay the baptism of children who have not completed their seventh year of age in order that they may receive special instructions. If, however, in a particular case a child attains the use of reason before that age, then he should receive some instruction.[67]

The length of time for instructions in ordinary cases may be legislated by diocesan statute, as was done in the first Synod of Fargo in 1941.[68] Ayrinhac (1867-1930), without mentioning the particular instruction, stated that the Sacred Congregation for the Propagation of the Faith urged that the period of instructions should last at least forty days. Again, without making any direct reference, he stated that a Synod of Nagasaki demanded that the period of the catechumenate last for two or three months, while the Synod of Pekin (1880) requested that a full year of study be given to the preparation for baptism.[69] In the absence of any diocesan regulation, the necessary period of time for convert in-

---

[62] *Theologia Moralis* (9. ed., 2 vols., Friburgi Brisgoviae, 1898), II, 59.

[63] Canon 88, § 3.

[64] Canon 745, § 2, 2°.

[65] De Clercq, *Traité de Droit Canonique,* II, n. 28.

[66] De Clercq, *loc. cit.*

[67] *The Homiletic and Pastoral Review,* XXXVI (1935-1936), 293 and 525.

[68] N. 214: "Neo-conversi per tres plus minusve menses, secundum personarum necessitates, duabus horis per hebdomadam de doctrina Catholica bene edoceantur."

[69] *Legislation on the Sacraments,* p. 30.

structions may be regulated by the pastor or the priest under whom the adult is receiving these instructions.[70]

The Church has not definitely determined the course of instructions to be imparted to the catechumen for the purpose of disposing and preparing him properly for the reception of the sacrament. From the common practice of the Church, however, it can be concluded that a complete instruction in Catholic doctrine, especially on the articles contained in the Profession of Faith, should be given. In the event that these instructions cannot be completely given before baptism, then the catechumen should be taught the basic truths, with the sincere promise that his course in Catholic doctrine will be completed after baptism.[71] In regard to the course of these instructions, the *Roman Ritual* states that the catechumen should be instructed "in the Christian Faith and holy manners."[72] By *Christian Faith* Augustine understood the truths to be believed *necessitate medii,* the existence of God, His remunerative justice, the Blessed Trinity and the Incarnation. He also added that a belief in Jesus Christ[73] and in the essential doctrines of Christian belief, which are contained in the Apostles' Creed, should be achieved through the instructions.[74]

Moreover, the Ten Commandments, the Lord's Prayer, and a knowledge of the sacraments should be taught to the catechumen.[75] Vermeersch stated that although the instructions which embrace all precepts of the divine law should regularly be completed before the conferring of baptism, yet the instructions concerning certain mysteries, such as the Holy Eucharist, may be postponed until after baptism, should circumstances require this arrangement.[76]

---

[70] Sipos, *Enchiridion Iuris Canonici* (3. ed., Pécs: ex Typographia "Haladàs R. T.," 1936), p. 424, footnote 17.

[71] Goodwine, *The Reception of Converts,* The Catholic University of America Canon Law Studies, n. 198 (Washington, D. C.: The Catholic University of America Press, 1944), p. 62.

[72] Tit. II, cap. 3, n. 1.

[73] S. C. S. Off. (Quebec), 10 mai 1703, n. 2—*Fontes,* n. 765.

[74] Augutine, *A Commentary on the New Code of Canon Law,* IV, 58.

[75] Goodwine, *op. cit.,* p. 66.

[76] Vermeersch-Creusen, *Epitome Iuris Canonici,* II, n. 34.

Art. 2. Adults in Danger of Death

The Church, in its sincere desire to have all souls obtain eternal salvation, requires but a minimum of instruction for a dying, yet conscious adult. As a consequence, the element of time normally demanded in the catechumenate for instructions preliminary to the reception of baptism has no place in the hasty though substantial preparation required for those who are baptized while in danger of death.

When an adult is in danger of death and cannot be diligently instructed in all the principal mysteries of the faith, then it is sufficient, in order that he may be baptized, that he assent in some manner to these doctrines, and sincerely promise that he will observe the commandments of the faith.[77] It would certainly be sufficient in such circumstances if he explicitly declared that he believed all the truths which the Catholic Church proposes for belief, or which the faithful believe, or whatever must be professed for his eternal salvation.[78] When a case of prudent doubt exists, and there is no time for further instructions, then baptism may be given conditionally with the formula *si es capax*. In the case of a semi-conscious patient the Holy Office stated that signs such as a nodding of the head or a simple "yes" are satisfactory when, at some time previous to the danger of death, the patient had expressed a desire of being baptized.[79]

Concerning a case of baptism in danger of death, the Sacred Congregation of the Holy Office was asked whether all the mysteries of the faith had to be explained to an adult who is near death, if such an instruction would disturb his peace of mind. In this inquiry it was suggested that a promise be obtained from the adult to the effect that he would complete the instruction if he should recover from the danger. In its reply the Holy Office stated that a mere promise was not sufficient from an adult who was capable of understanding the principal doctrines of the Church, and that, consequently, the mysteries of the faith which were req-

[77] Canon 752, § 2.

[78] Coronata, *De Sacramentis,* I, n. 131.

[79] S. C. S. Off. (Perth.), 18 sept. 1850, n. 2—*Fontes,* n. 912; S. C. S. Off. (Mission. Loang. et Kacong.), 8 mart. 1770, n. 1—*Fontes,* n. 827.

uisite as a means were to be imparted to him, even when he was near death.[80]

If a person has fallen into complete unconsciousness and can no longer ask for baptism, but has either previously or in his present state manifested his desire to receive baptism, he can be baptized conditionally with the formula *si vis baptizari.* In the event of his recovery if some doubt remains concerning the validity of his previous baptism, then he should be rebaptized conditionally with the formula: *si non es baptizatus.*[81] Vermeersch stated that conditional baptism should be given to an adult who is dying and who cannot in any way manifest his mind, even though he may have resisted conversion while he was in good health.[82] But this doctrine appears to be at variance with the Code, which requires either the present existence of an intention to receive baptism, or a previous manifestation of the same.[83] Since in the case of an adult the intention to receive baptism is necessary for the validity of the sacrament,[84] it must be concluded that under the circumstances proposed by Vermeersch the sacrament would be exposed to invalidity in a very haphazard manner.

SECT. III. THE TIME OF BAPTISM IN REGARD TO INFANTS

Art. 1. Infants Must Be Baptized "Quamprimum"

Since the danger of dying without baptism is much more present for infants than for adults, and since infants are capable of receiving only baptism of water, whereas adults may receive baptism of desire, the Church urges with much more insistence the foregoing of all delay in the baptism of infants.[85] In legislating concerning the baptism of infants, the Code explicitly states that

---

[80] S. C. S. Off. (Quebec), 25 ian. 1703, n. 2—*Fontes,* n. 764.

[81] Canon 752, § 3.

[82] Vermeersch, *Theologiae Moralis Principia, Responsa, Consilia* (3. ed., 4 vols., Roma: Università Gregoriana, 1933-1937), III, n. 243 (hereafter cited *Theologiae Moralis*); Vermeersch-Creusen, *Epitome Iuris Canonici,* II, n. 35.

[83] Canon 752, § 2.

[84] Coronata, *De Sacramentis,* I, n. 131.

[85] Lehmkuhl, *Theologia Moralis,* II, 60.

they shall be baptized *"quamprimum,"* without in any way indicating how long a period of time is embraced by this term. Since a number of factors must be considered in relation to the baptism of infants, it appears that the Church does not wish to make as part of its general law a rigid determination of time for infant baptism.

The opinions of moralists and canonists vary concerning the length of the period of time and the gravity of the obligation involved. Genicot (1856-1900) was of the opinion that a notable delay of time in the baptism of an infant is not a morally grave matter as long as there is no serious intention of entirely neglecting the baptism, provided, however, that the delay is not accompanied with any danger of death.[86] Noldin also held this opinion in the early editions of his work,[87] but in recent editions of his work that doctrine has been completely retracted.[88] Since the time the law of the Code came into effect, most of the authors consider it a violation of a grave obligation when the baptism of an infant is delayed for a notable period of time without a just cause.[89]

Just what constitutes a notable period of time is rather difficult to ascertain. If the threat of public scandal and the danger of death for the infant are not present, it becomes almost impossible to indicate in what specific period of time the baptism of a child is demanded as the fulfillment of a grave obligation.[90] Benedict XIV (1740-1758) stated that the baptism of an infant should not be delayed beyond eight days,[91] and Leo XIII (1878-1903) considered the deferring of baptism of infants for weeks and months as contrary to ecclesiastical law.[92] The Sacred Congregation for the Propagation of the Faith considered the term *quam-*

---

[86] *Institutiones Theologiae Moralis,* II, n. 146.

[87] *Summa Theologiae Moralis* (5. ed., Oeniponte: Typis et Sumptibus Fel. Rauch, F. Pustet, 1904-1905), III, n. 72.

[88] Noldin-Schmitt, *Summa Theologiae Moralis,* III, n. 73.

[89] Cappello, *De Sacramentis,* I, n. 149; Noldin, *Summa Theologiae Moralis,* III, n. 66; Vermeersch-Creusen, *Epitome Iuris Canonici,* II n., 52.

[90] Prümmer, *Manuale Theologiae Moralis,* III, n. 126.

[91] *De Synodo Dioecesana Libri XIII* (2 vols., Parmae: ex Typographia Fratrum Borsi, 1764), Lib. XII, cap. 6, n. 7—Vol. II, p. 98.

[92] Ep. *Gratiae,* 22 iul. 1899—*Fontes,* n. 641.

primum to signify three or, at most, eight days from the birth of the child.[93]

Among the more recent authors, some state that it is a grave obligation to have an infant baptized within ten or eleven days,[94] while others believe that the obligation of infant baptism must be fulfilled within ten to fifteen days after birth, and at the most within one month, even in the absence of any threat of scandal or any danger of death.[95] In the opinion of Coronata, the delay should not exceed fifteen days, even granted that there is no danger of death.[96] But Barrett (1862-1935) allowed the deferment of infant baptism to extend to a period of three weeks, but not beyond it without a just cause.[97]

According to St. Alphonsus (1696-1787)[98] a number of authors considered the notable period of time requiring infant baptism under grave obligation to be a month. If, however, there existed a just cause for further delay, then the period of time could be extended to two months at the most.[99] This opinion seems now to command the greater probability in view of the fact that the term *"quamprimum"* cannot be determined with absolute exactness, but is rather to be understood in a relative sense, especially since the factors of distance, climate, and the health of the child may easily cause a delay of several days or a few weeks. As a relative norm, *quamprimum* implies that the duration of time within which infant baptism is to be conferred in fulfillment of a grave obligation is of a somewhat elastic character. Thus the period of time

[93] Litt. S. C. de Prop. Fide (ad Vic. Ap. Coreae), 11 sept. 1841—*Collectanea S. Congregationis de Propaganda Fide,* n. 939.

[94] E.g., Aertnys-Damen, *Theologia Moralis* (13. ed., 2 vols., Taurini: Marietti, 1939), II, n. 55.

[95] Merkelbach, *Summa Theologiae Moralis,* III, n. 148.

[96] *De Sacramentis,* I, n. 151.

[97] Sabetti-Barrett, *Compendium Theologiae Moralis,* I, p. 584.

[98] *Theologia Moralis,* lib. VI, n. 118 (2 vols., Taurini: Marietti, 1878), II, p. 185.

[99] Prümmer, *Manuale Theologiae Moralis,* III, n. 126; Lehmkuhl, *Theologia Moralis,* II, 60; Vermeersch-Creusen, *Epitome Iuris Canonici,* II, n. 52; Woywod, *A Practical Commentary on the Code of Canon Law,* I, 669; Claeys Bouuaert-Simenon, *Manuale Juris Canonici* (3 vols., Vol. II, Gandae et Leodii: Dessain, 1931), II, n. 50.

will vary somewhat from one case to the next, so that any reasonable cause would permit a delay of the administration of baptism beyond the more usual period of time. The cause, however, would have to be graver in proportion as the delay becomes longer.[100]

But this term of duration is not so elastic as to allow an extremely long deferment or even an indefinite delay. Consequently, since in ordinary circumstances a month is considered the maximum amount of time for deferring the baptism of an infant, a reasonable cause will proportionately permit a delay of infant baptism for even as long as two months. Beyond this a delay cannot be tolerated. This doctrine seems in accord with the preference expressed by the Sacred Congregation for the Propagation of the Faith. If some special cause seems to demand a delay of baptism beyond two months, then private baptism should be conferred in place of any further wait for solemn baptism. The Congregation considered such a case one of emergency or necessity.[101]

There are various reasonable causes which permit a delay of baptism from one to two months. Such a cause would exist when the family lives a long distance from the church, and adequate means of transportation are not at the time available to them. Perhaps it may be a case of risking travel for some distance over icy and hazardous roads. In such circumstances a delay longer than a month would be warranted in the awaiting of a warmer temperature that would render travel somewhat safer. Again, a delay could be occasioned by cold or stormy weather which might endanger the infant's health, if he is exposed to it very early after birth. There could also be a case in which the infant is affected with a peculiar condition of health, which in no way places him in danger of death, but which might be seriously aggravated by travel. All these cases would furnish reasonable causes for deferring baptism to a period of almost two months. Never, however, is it allowed to delay baptism over a month in order to accommodate the wishes of parents, who are awaiting the arrival

---

[100] Claeys Bouuaert-Simenon, *op. cit.*, II, n. 50.

[101] S. C. de Prop. Fide, instr., 31 iul. 1902—*Collectanea S. Congregationis de Propaganda Fide,* n. 2149.

of godparents living at a far distance, and unable to come within a month after birth.[102]

Although the general law does not absolutely indicate the period of time that fits the notion of *quamprimum,* it is within the power of the bishop to determine by diocesan statute the exact number of days within which the grave obligation of baptizing infants must be fulfilled. In making this regulation, the bishop should, in his prudent judgment, have a thorough knowledge of the conditions existing in his diocese, which might warrant an exact determination of the time of baptism after an infant's birth. In certain dioceses the difficulty of bringing the child to the parish because of bad roads or adverse climate might warrant the extension of the period of time required for baptism to a period longer than that normally understood as *quamprimum.*[103]

By diocesan legislation the bishop can command that baptism should not be deferred even beyond the short space of eight days.[104] In cases in which undue hardship would be imposed by this legislation, special allowance should be made. Mothon stated that in a certain number of dioceses in France there are synodal statutes or episcopal ordinances prohibiting the delay of the administration of baptism to infants beyond a week after birth in the absence of any motivating cause. If the delay in the baptism be not accompanied with such a cause, then all the customary solemnities attached to the administration of baptism in that country, such as the playing of the organ or the ringing of bells, are prohibited.[105] In view of the fact that in ordinary cases the maximum amount of time for deferring infant baptism is about one month, Cappello states that diocesan laws permitting the delay of the sacrament beyond a month are contrary to the common

---

[102] S. C. S. Off., 11 ian. 1899—*Fontes,* n. 1214.

[103] Claeys Bouuaert-Simenon, *op. cit.,* II, n. 50; Lehmkuhl, *Theologia Moralis,* II, 60; Merkelbach, *Summa Theologiae Moralis,* III, n. 148; Cappello, *De Sacramentis,* I, n. 141.

[104] Vermeersch-Creusen, *Epitome Iuris Canonici,* II, n. 52; Coronata, *De Sacramentis,* I, n. 151.

[105] *Institutions Canoniques* (3 vols., Paris: Desclée, de Brouwer et Cie, 1922-1924), II, art. 1702.

law and should be corrected.[106] Of course, as has been stated above, extraordinary circumstances will permit the deferring of baptism for more than a month to be made part of the diocesan legislation.

In conjunction with the law requiring the baptism of infants *quamprimum,* the pastor and confessors are exhorted to inform parents of their obligation of having their children baptized within a short period of time after birth lest otherwise they delay it without an urgent cause, and expose their children to the danger of dying without the sacrament.[107] This counsel for parents can be given in religious instructions, especially in a course of sermons given at regular intervals on the sacraments.[108] In speaking on baptism, the parish priests can insist that parents should not defer the baptism of infants for the reason simply that the godparents cannot come until after the lapse of a considerable period of time. In such cases the parents should call on the sponsors to select proxies for the godparents. Moreover, Lenten preachers and priests who conduct missions and novenas should denounce with special vehemence the great abuse of unnecessarily deferring baptism for a long time.[109]

So important is this duty of parents that the Holy See has urged bishops in their quinquennial report to indicate whether parents generally presented their children for baptism within a week after birth, or whether they deferred the administration of the sacrament for a long period of time.[110] In conclusion, parents should be instructed that they have the grave obligation of having their children baptized at least within a month after birth, and

---

[106] *De Sacramentis,* I, n. 141.

[107] Prümmer, *Manuale Theologiae Moralis,* III, n. 126.

[108] O'Kane-Fallon, *Notes on the Rubrics of the Roman Ritual* (new edition completely revised in accordance with the latest 1925 *Editio Typica* of the *Rituale Romanum* and the Decrees of the Sacred Congregation, Dublin: James Duffy and Co., Ltd., 1938), n. 131.

[109] De Clercq, *Traité de Droit Canonique,* II, n. 53.

[110] S. C. Consist., decr. 31 dec. 1909, cap. XI, n. 118—*Fontes,* n. 206; *De Relationibus Dioecesanis,* cap. XI, n. 86—*Acta Apostolica Sedis Commentarium Officiale* (Romae: 1909-), X (1918), 501 (hereafter referred to as *AAS*).

that only for a reasonable cause and under extraordinary circumstances may they defer baptism from one to two months.

Art. 2. The Delay of Infant Baptism

Among some pastors there is the practice of deferring for a determined or even indefinite time the baptism of infants offered by indifferent or lapsed Catholics. Through this practice it is hoped that the parents who have lapsed from their practice of their faith may be awakened to the fact of their negligence and spurred on to a stricter performance of their duties. A repeated neglect regarding the fulfillment of the Easter duty would brand such parents as non-practicing Catholics and accordingly would bar their children from the non-delayed reception of infant baptism.

In regard to Catholic parents who have lapsed from the habitual performance of their duties, one might make a division into four groups: (1) those who are living in an invalid marriage for which there is no remedy in the face of some existing impediment that cannot be removed through a dispensation; (2) those who are living in an invalid marriage which can be validated; (3) those who are validly married in a Catholic marriage, but have become indifferent to their religious duties and practices; and (4) those who are validly married in a mixed marriage, but the Catholic party has become a non-practicing member of the faith. If the parents of any one of these four groups offer their children for baptism, it cannot be said that they have completely lost all regard for their Catholic duties and practices. To some extent they feel that they are Catholics of some sort, at least in name; otherwise they would not want their children baptized.

As a consequence, they cannot be classified as heretics, apostates or schismatics,[111] who indeed are entitled to present their children for baptism as long as they give a sufficient guarantee that their children will be reared and educated in the Catholic religion.[112] In consideration of these facts, therefore, it follows *a fortiori* that

[111] Canon 1325.

[112] Canon 751.

the minimum required for the lawful baptism of the children of non-Catholics will apply to the baptism of children who are presented by non-practicing Catholic parents.[113] Thus, when these parents offer their children for baptism, it seems proper that they be baptized under the usual conditions demanded for the baptism of the children of non-Catholics, the assurance of the Catholic education of the children.

There are, nevertheless, those who believe that in the case of lapsed Catholics the baptism of their children should be delayed until a time when the parents return to the practice of the Catholic faith. With good reason these nominal Catholics can be considered as incompetent to rear their children in the Catholic faith, since they themselves have no regard for their own obligations. Their personal indifference in most cases, it is argued, cannot help but influence their manner of rearing their children, so that they will have little conscientious regard for Catholic education and discipline. Furthermore, the indifferent attitude of the parents will often serve as a norm upon which their children will base their lives.

There is much to be said for such reasoning. But it would be unfair to apply such arguments in the case of the children of parents living in a bad marriage which cannot in any way be validated in the face of an impediment for which no dispensation can be conceded. These parents may often be very desirous of seeing their children reared in an atmosphere redolent of Catholic truths and practices, though they themselves have unfortunately relinquished the practice of their faith.

In regard to those who are living in a bad marriage which can be validated, or who are validly married but indifferent to the Catholic faith, the deferring of the baptism of their children will result in one of two reactions. Either they will realize the horror of their sinful lives and strive to rectify the situation, or they will interpret the refusal of baptism as a punishment for their failure to practice their faith, and thus they will grow more obstinate in their way of life.

---

[113] "Baptizing Children of Lapsed Parents," *The Clergy Review* (London, 1931—), XXV (1945), 370.

Whatever mode of procedure be adopted in these cases must certainly be in accord with the mind of the Church. It is true that the Church does not legislate for such cases; rather, it looks explicitly to the children of infidels,[114] heretics, apostates and schismatics.[115] The case of lapsed or indifferent Catholics is not directly touched in the Code, for canon 770 gives an absolute rule for the baptism of the children of all Catholics. Hence one must seek to resolve the question by resorting to canon 20, which states that in the absence of any express prescript of the law the norm must be taken from the general principles of law, from the style and practice of the Roman Curia, or from the common and constant teaching of the doctors. Since the law in no way treats directly of the matter, the mind of the Church must be considered as expressed in the style and practice of the Roman Curia.[116]

The practice of the Church, as indicated on several occasions in the decrees of the Holy Office,[117] is that children of indifferent or tepid parents can and ought to be baptized when these parents request it, and give promise of rearing the children in the Catholic faith.[118] Even though the parents are living in a sinful union, yet this will not justify the delay of baptism, since the parents may have every intention of rearing the child in the Catholic faith, especially when sufficient assurance regarding the Catholic education of the child is given.[119]

Since the children are the innocent victims in the case, the Church does not wish to deprive them of baptism when there is

---

[114] Canon 750.

[115] Canon 751.

[116] Oesterle, "De Baptismo Infantium e Tepidis Catholicis Progenitorum," *Jus Pontificium* (Romae, 1921-1940), XVIII (1938), 186-191.

[117] S. C. S. Off., 18 nov. 1745, ad 1—*Fontes,* n. 746; S. C. S. Off., 14 oct. 1676 ad 2—*Collectanea S. Congregationis de Propaganda Fide,* n. 211.

[118] S. C. de Prop. Fide (C. P. pro Sin.—Sutchuen.), 31 ian. 1796: "Concludendem, parentum fidelium tepiditatem aut alterius eorumdem pravae agendi rationis considerationem, non obesse quominus, postulantibus praesertim ipsimet parentibus, ut in proposito casu, rite illorum infantes baptizari valeant ac debeant."—*Collectanea S. Congregationis de Propaganda Fide,* n. 625.

[119] "A Pastor's Refusal of Baptism," *ER,* LXXXVII (1932), 524-526.

any possibility under the ecclesiastical law of permitting the administration of the sacrament in these circumstances. The very fact that the child is presented for baptism seems to indicate some faith in the parents, and this is also some guarantee that the children will be reared as Catholics.[120] This guarantee does not postulate the moral certainty which is demanded before a matrimonial dispensation from mixed religion may be granted.[121] In 1898 the Holy Office stated simply that a *possible hope* concerning the Catholic education of the child was sufficient, and that baptism should be refused only when this hope was missing.[122]

It seems that the hope of converting these indifferent Catholic parents from their sinful lives to a sense of responsibility of their Catholic duties and obligations is the reason why the Church has enacted that a priest should baptize their child, even though there may be only little hope that the child will be reared in the Catholic faith.[123] There are exceptions, however, in which there is evident proof that the Catholic education of the child will be neglected. When such cases present themselves, then baptism may be deferred for even an indefinite time. For these cases Pope Benedict XIV did not give any absolute rule, but left the decision to the prudence and discretion of the ordinary concerned.[124]

As a consequence, it may be stated that the Church wishes the children of careless and indifferent Catholics to be baptized as soon as possible, provided there is a possible hope that the children will be reared as Catholics. It is not necessary, therefore, to be concerned with remote dangers, but only with the proximate dangers that may exist. A *possible hope* removes to some extent, though not entirely, this proximate danger to the child's Catholic training.

---

[120] Woywod, "Baptism of Infants of Parents Whose Marriage is Invalid," *Homiletic and Pastoral Review,* XXIV (1924), 1063.

[121] Canon 1061, § 1, 3°.

[122] S. C. S. Off., 6 iul. 1898, ad 4: "Si possibilis spes affulgeat fore ut huiusmodi pueri possint suo tempore in vera religione institui, tunc, datis cautionibus, baptizentur. Quod si nulla via possit huiusmodi spes moralis haberi, tunc, nisi pueri in mortis articulo inveniantur, ab iis baptizandis abstineatur."—*Fontes,* n. 1200.

[123] Woywod, *A Practical Commentary on the Code of Canon Law,* I, n. 644.

[124] Benedictus XIV, ep. encycl., *Inter omnigenas,* 2 febr. 1744, n. 8—*Fontes,* n. 339.

By such a broad permission the Church indicates that there is always some hope of amendment on the part of indifferent Catholics. Such a case is not analogous to that in which both parents are non-Catholics, for nominal Catholics admit in principle, though not in fact, the truths of the Catholic faith which are denied by Protestants. Moreover, even though the child's Catholic education may later be neglected, yet he is likely to have a conscious conviction of his responsibility to God as a Catholic, either amid the afflictions of life or at the hour of death. Such a Catholic would indeed be more apt to seek the ministration of a priest at the hour of death than one who is not baptized a Catholic.[125]

With regard to children one of whose parents is a non-Catholic and the other a lapsed Catholic, the Church benignly applies the same rule as that adopted in the case of parents who are both lapsed Catholics. As long as the priest judges in such a case that there is some possible hope that the child will be reared in the Catholic faith, the child should be baptized without delay.[126] This is especially true if the mother, who is a lapsed Catholic, offers the child for baptism.[127] Even if the Catholic parent in such a marriage is dead, nevertheless the child's baptism should not be delayed, as long as this hope of a Catholic education exists.[128]

Hence the Church does not condone any general practice of deferring the baptism of children of lapsed Catholics for either a definite or an indefinite period of time. Provided there are present some guarantees of a future Catholic instruction, the Church considers these sufficient, for it certainly would be a strange procedure to demand more from indifferent Catholics than from non-Catholics, who have no knowledge of or only little acquaintance with Catholic truths. Of course, local ecclesiastical authority will often indicate the course to be followed.[129] But this will in general harmonize with the mind of the Church in this matter.

---

[125] "Is it Lawful to Baptize the Children of Catholics Who Implicitly Deny their Faith?" *ER,* XX (1899), 297.

[126] Claeys Bouuaert-Simenon, *Manuale Juris Canonici,* II, n. 32.

[127] Cappello, *De Sacramentis,* I, n. 144.

[128] Coronata, *De Sacramentis,* I, n. 129.

[129] De Clercq, *Traité de Droit Canonique,* II, n. 27.

In conclusion, it is in agreement with pastoral prudence not to defer the baptism of children of lapsed Catholic parents when they are brought by these parents or by Catholic sponsors with the parents' consent, provided there is expressed a willingness, which is accompanied with at least some possible hope, that the children will be reared and educated in the Catholic faith.

CHAPTER V

Time and Place of Baptism in Cases of Necessity

SECT. I. PRIVATE BAPTISM FOR INFANTS AND ADULTS

Solemn baptism is the administration of the sacrament with all the rites and ceremonies which are prescribed in the liturgical books. On the other hand, private or non-solemn baptism is simply the conferring of baptism without these accompanying rites and ceremonies.[1] Essentially the form is the same, but there can be a difference in the matter in so far as baptismal water, blessed for sacramental purposes, is required for the administration of solemn baptism, while ordinary water may be employed in private baptism.[2] Necessity, determined by existing conditions, can make the use of ordinary or blessed water equally as lawful as baptismal water.[3] In preference to common water, however, holy water should always be employed if it is near at hand.[4] If it is possible, baptismal water should be kept available in a hospital, especially when baptisms are frequent.[5]

In the case of adults who are converted from heresy and are baptized conditionally, private baptism may be conferred.[6] Otherwise private baptism cannot be conferred on either adults or infants except in a case of urgent necessity.[7] Such a case of urgent necessity implies that no particular time or season is set aside for the conferring of private baptism, inasmuch as necessity is not confined to any definite time of the year or day. When the circum-

---

[1] Canon 737, § 2.

[2] Augustine, *A Commentary on the New Code of Canon Law,* IV, 35.

[3] "Private Baptism," *ER,* LXXV (1926), 308-309.

[4] S. C. S. Off., 20 iun. 1883—*Fontes,* n. 1082.

[5] Drumm, *Hospital Chaplains,* The Catholic University of America Canon Law Studies, n. 178 (Washington, D. C.: The Catholic University of America Press, 1943), p. 114.

[6] Canon 759, § 2.

[7] Canon 771.

stance of necessity demands the immediate conferring of the sacrament, then that is the suitable time for the administration of private baptism. Thus private baptism can be conferred at any time, provided there exists the corresponding necessity.

Just what constitutes the *necessitas urgens* is a matter variously explained according to divergent opinions. The Code states that private baptism can be conferred in danger of death,[8] and that outside the danger of death private baptism cannot be given, except in the case of an adult converted from heresy.[9] Thus the statement of the Code seems to be absolute and to leave no room for other existing circumstances that could warrant the administration of private baptism. In every other case, except for the danger of death and the conditional baptism of an adult convert, it seems from the Code that private baptism could indeed be conferred validly, but only illicitly. This, however, is not in complete accord with the decrees of the Holy See, which allowed a wider extension of the circumstances for the administration of private baptism.

In view of the situation in missionary countries, where the priest is often absent from a given group of his people while he goes a far distance to minister to another group, the Sacred Congregation for the Propagation of the Faith permitted catechists to baptize the children of Christians when a priest was not present in the territory or could not be reached elsewhere within ten days after the birth of the child.[10] This permission for the conferring of private baptism was conceded not so much because of the fact that a real danger of death existed, but because of the fact that a priest would not be present in the vicinity for a long time. Since baptism should be conferred as soon as possible,[11] and since only a priest,[12] or a deacon[13] can confer solemn baptism, the Congregation permitted a catechist to confer private baptism. Since the

---

[8] Canon 759, § 1.

[9] Canon 759, § 2.

[10] (C. P. pro Sin.), 21 ian. 1788—*Fontes,* n. 4618 (C. P. Pro Sin. Cochinchin.), 16 ian. 1804—*Fontes,* n. 4677; litt. (ad Vic. Ap. Coreae), 11 sept. 1841—*Fontes,* n. 4795.

[11] Canon 770.

[12] Canon 738, § 1.

[13] Canon 741.

Sacred Congregation was really concerned with the needs of mission countries when this enactment was decreed, these decisions and others concerning permission for the conferring of private baptism[14] are to be interpreted as applying only to missionary territory, and not to regions where the Catholic Church has already been well organized.[15]

Nevertheless, the case of *urgent necessity* contemplated in canon 771 can entail more than just a danger of death in reference to the lawful administration of private baptism even in our own country or in other similar regions. Thus, if unjust civil laws interfered with the freedom of religion, so that a priest could not confer solemn baptism without suffering a penalty, or if a religious persecution was raging, then private baptism could be lawfully administered by some member of the laity in any convenient and suitable place.[16] There may also exist the rare and extreme case in which the father absolutely and with menacing threats refuses, in opposition to the strong desires of the mother, to have his child baptized. Even in the absence of the father it may be impossible to have the child solemnly baptized by the priest, inasmuch as there are others who might easily reveal this fact to him. In such a case, for the eternal salvation of the child and for the peace of soul of the mother, the child could be given private baptism.[17]

In administering the sacrament, the priest on a rare occasion may be urged by necessity to confer only private baptism, when it is a case in which indeed the parents desire baptism for the child, but stubbornly oppose the use of the prescribed ceremonies and rites. Or again it may be a case in which the holy oils and the salt could not be obtained in consequence of some calamity or disaster.[18] In practice, however, in non-missionary territory private

---

[14] S. C. de Prop. Fide (C. G.-Antiban.), 28 nov. 1785—*Fontes,* n. 4609; S. C. de Prop. Fide (C. P. pro Sin.), 21 ian. 1789, n. 1—*Fontes,* n. 4625.

[15] Merkelbach, *Summa Theologiae Moralis,* III, n. 139; Vermeersch-Creusen, *Epitome Iuris Canonici,* II, n. 25; Cappello, *De Sacramentis,* I, n. 138; Waldron, *The Minister of Baptism,* p. 137.

[16] Cappello, *De Sacramentis,* I, n. 138.

[17] Genicot, *Institutiones Theologiae Moralis,* II, n. 740.

[18] Augustine, *A Commentary on the New Code of Canon Law,* IV, 71.

baptism will usually be conferred simply in a danger of death, and only rarely in other extreme circumstances.

It is not necessary that there be present a certain or absolute danger of death in order that the conferring of private baptism may be undertaken licitly. All that is required is that there exist here and now a probable danger of death, even if the basis of this probability consists simply in a reasonable fear.[19] Since necessity knows no law, private baptism may be administered in any place.[20] But since private baptism will usually be conferred when a person is in danger of death, it will happen most frequently that private baptism will be conferred at the home or in a hospital. Nevertheless, since the danger of death can emerge in any circumstance, any place will be suitable and proper for the conferring of private baptism.

Moreover, inasmuch as baptism will often be administered by a doctor or a nurse to an infant, or less frequently to an adult, in danger of death, the chaplain of a hospital or the pastor of the parish in which the hospital is located should from time to time investigate whether those upon whom this grave duty may fall are really conversant with the correct and valid manner of conferring private baptism. Thus he should inquire whether they know what is needed for valid matter and what is required for the correct form.[21]

If, perchance, they lack the proper knowledge required for conferring a valid baptism, then the chaplain should instruct the personnel concerning the circumstances in which they are allowed to administer private baptism. Besides, he should instruct them concerning the proper matter and form of the sacrament and the procedure in administering it. Quite definitely he should inculcate in them a sense of the special importance of giving immediate notification to the chaplain, when a patient is in danger of death.[22] After the actual administration of every private baptism by a doctor or a nurse, the chaplain or pastor should make sure that everything

---

[19] Merkelbach, *Summa Theologiae Moralis,* III, n. 139.

[20] Canon 771.

[21] Prümmer, *Manuale Theologiae Moralis,* III, n. 123.

[22] Drumm, *Hospital Chaplains,* p. 115.

required for the validity of the sacrament was present.[23] In regard, however, to private baptism conferred in Catholic hospitals, there will generally be little or no justification for doubting its validity, since the hospital's personnel is well instructed concerning the proper time for the conferring of private baptism and the correct manner of its administration.[24]

SECT. II. EMERGENCY BAPTISM

Art. 1. Baptism of the Unborn

Not infrequently there may occur a case of extreme necessity that calls for the private baptism of an unborn child who is in danger of death. In the past some held the opinion that the proper time for baptism was only after the birth of a child and not previous to it, otherwise they considered the baptism as invalid. Those who maintained this opinion relied on the argument that no one can be born again spiritually through baptism prior to the time of the physical birth.[25] Nevertheless, the opposite opinion can also be supported from Sacred Scripture,[26] so that one may be said, in a theological sense, to be "born" when one is conceived in the womb.[27]

Moreover, since in the days of St. Thomas the medical profession had not devised means of reaching an infant while it was in the uterus, he held that the body of an infant could not be baptized, since it could not be touched by water.[28] But the opposite opinion can now be well sustained, since doctors can easily, by means of special instruments, reach the body of an infant while it is still in the womb.[29]

Today it is commonly held that in a case of danger of death one should not wait until the time of actual birth for the con-

[23] Prümmer, *op. cit.,* III, n. 123.

[24] Drumm, *op. cit.,* p. 115.

[25] John, III:5.

[26] Matt., I:20: "Quod enim in ea natum est, de Spiritu Sancto est."

[27] O'Kane, *Notes on the Rubrics of the Roman Ritual,* n. 196.

[28] *Summa Theologica,* Pars III, q. LXVIII, a. 10: "Corpus infantis antequam nascatur ex utero, non potest aliquo modo ablui aqua."

[29] Blat, *Commentarium,* Lib. III, Pars I, n. 30.

ferring of baptism, but that one should undertake the administration of baptism in the womb, at least conditionally.[30] Because of the difficulty, however, of having absolute assurance in all cases of the flow of water on the head, there can exist some degree of doubt concerning the valid administration of baptism. Therefore, the Sacred Congregation of the Council decreed that, if an infant was baptized in the womb, he should be conditionally baptized after birth.[31] Even if the doctor testifies that the water touched the head while the infant was still in the uterus, nevertheless, after its birth the infant must again, i.e., conditionally, be baptized.[32]

Since it is illicit to resort to a doubtful in place of a valid administration of a sacrament, an infant may not be baptized in the womb as long as there exists a probable hope that the infant can be baptized when born.[33] Before all probable hope of a normal baptism will be lacking in any particular case, there must be present a reasonable fear that the child will die before its birth. This fear of the unborn infant's death can be occasioned by such factors as a protracted labor, a difficult presentation, a constricted pelvis, hydrocephalus, and eclampsia.[34]

For a valid baptism the water must flow directly upon the fetus. A valid baptism cannot be conferred on the unruptured membrane of a fetus, for this membrane is really not part of the body of the infant.[35] As a consequence, baptism cannot be administered in

---

[30] Coronata, *De Sacramentis,* I, n. 125; Noldin-Schmitt, *Summa Theologiae Moralis,* III, n. 71; Vermeersch-Creusen, *Epitome Iuris Canonici,* II, n. 30; Claeys Bouuaert-Simenon, *Manuale Juris Canonici,* II, n. 28; Blat, *op. cit.,* lib. III, pars I, n. 30; Merkelbach, *Summa Theologiae Moralis,* III, n. 154; Prümmer, *Manuale Theologiae Moralis,* III, n. 129; Davis, *Moral and Pastoral Theology* (4. ed., 4 vols., New York: Sheed and Ward, 1945), III, 49.

[31] S. C. C., *Sutrina,* 12 iul. 1794—*Fontes,* n. 3890.

[32] Prümmer, *op. cit.,* III, n. 129.

[33] Canon 746, § 1.

[34] McAllister, *Emergency Baptism* (Milwaukee: Bruce Publishing Company, 1945), n. 37.

[35] Capellmann, *Medicina Pastoralis* (7. ed., Aquisgrani: Rudolphus Barth, 1890), p. 103; Bonnar, *The Catholic Doctor* (2. ed., New York: P. J. Kenedy and Sons, 1939), p. 94.

the womb, unless the membranes are ruptured and the amniotic fluid discharged.[36] It is morally prohibited to rupture the membranes of an inviable fetus in order to administer baptism, because this is a direct attack upon the fetus, and a direct abortion is never permissible.[37] After the membranes of a viable fetus have been ruptured, baptism can be administered through the use of a sterile bulb, syringe, or other irrigating instrument to apply water, so that it may directly flow upon the body of the infant.[38]

Since it is the physician's responsibility to estimate whether danger of death exists, it is he who in the eventuality of this danger should confer the baptism in the uterus.[39] Although a priest, such as the hospital chaplain, were available, the baptism in the womb should be conferred not by him, but by the physician, not only at the demand of Christian decency, but also in the interests of a mode of operation that proves harmless for the mother the while it may prove helpful for the child.[40] Because of the fact that for reaching the infant's body a special precision is required, and since great harm could be inflicted on the mother through the improper use of the instruments, it is best that, whenever it is possible, if a physician is not available, then this duty should be performed by a skilled and capable nurse. In either case it should be arranged that a card containing the formula of baptism in clear type should be held before the minister while he confers uterine baptism.[41]

Doctors may use disinfectants, such as corrosive sublimate, by adding one part of the solution to a thousand parts of baptismal or other natural water. This is done with a view to preventing inflammation and to obviating the danger of contagion for the

---

[36] Merkelbach, *Summa Theologiae Moralis,* III, n. 156; McFadden, *Medical Ethics* (2. ed., Philadelphia: F. A. Davis Company, 1949), p. 238.

[37] McFadden, *op. cit.,* p. 239; Bonnar, *op. cit.,* p. 94.

[38] Merkelbach, *loc. cit.;* Claeys Bouuaert-Simenon, *Manuale Juris Canonici,* II, n. 28.

[39] McAllister, *Emergency Baptism,* n. 37.

[40] Cappello, *De Sacramentis,* I, n. 157; Bonnar, *op. cit.,* p 94.

[41] Bowen, *Baptism of the Infant and Fetus, an Outline for the Use of Doctors and Nurses* (4. ed., Dubuque: The M. J. Knippel Co., 1939), p. 7.

mother.[42] It is permitted to doctors and nurses in the absence of other more acceptable means to attempt uterine baptism by wetting the hand or finger and rubbing the forehead of the undelivered child with their hand or finger while they pronounce the conditional formula of baptism. This mode of baptism, however, is considered doubtful.[43]

In every case of uterine baptism, the sacrament should be administered conditionally: "If you are capable of receiving baptism, I baptize thee in the Name of the Father, and of the Son, and of the Holy Ghost." When the case is one of difficult delivery, however, and the head has appeared, baptism should be conferred absolutely on it and should not be repeated when the child is born.[44] When any other member of the body is presented, such as the hand, foot, shoulder, etc., baptism should be administered conditionally on the part presented. In case several parts are presented, baptism should be given on the part nearest the head. After birth the child must again be conditionally baptized.[45] Baptism conferred upon the umbilical cord would be invalid, since it is only a temporary part of the child.[46]

Art. 2. Baptism of the Premature Fetus

Ecclesiastical law decrees that every premature fetus must be baptized, no matter at what time during pregnancy it may have been discharged.[47] The word fetus as it is employed in the Code should be taken in the broadest sense to include an embryo or fertilized ovum.[48] Since the principal purpose of baptism is to cleanse the soul of original sin, and since the law enacts that a fetus in any stage of pregnancy must be baptized, it seems evident that ecclesiastical legislation favors the view that the soul "informs"

---

[42] S. C. S. Off., 21 aug. 1901—*Fontes,* n. 1256; "Private Baptism," *ER,* LXXV (1926), 308-309.

[43] S. C. S. Off., 14 dec. 1898—*Fontes,* n. 1211.

[44] Canon 746, § 2.

[45] Canon 746, § 3.

[46] McFadden, *Medical Ethics,* p. 239.

[47] Canon 747.

[48] Claeys Bouuaert-Simenon, *Manuale Juris Canonici,* II, n. 30.

the ovum at the very moment of conception. Today it is maintained by most of the theologians and the canonists that the soul is infused into the human ovum at the time of conception.[49]

Even today, however, there are a few who do not accept the theory of infusion of the soul immediately in conjunction with the fertilization of the human ovum.[50] Despite the fact, however, that the opinion which professes the immediate infusion of the soul is almost universally accepted, the decree of ecclesiastical law requiring the baptism of the fetus in any stage of development does not absolutely confirm this fact as a positive doctrine of the Church. Rather, since baptism is absolutely necessary for salvation, the Code furnishes a practical norm by which the eternal salvation of a possible soul is safely assured. Thus the Code in no way intends to make a theoretical declaration,[51] but it only wants to ensure the fulfillment of the obligation springing from the highest law of charity, which demands that baptism be administered as soon as possible to such a probably existing soul.[52]

It is often difficult to determine whether a fetus is living or not. Although signs of life cannot with certainty be discerned, nevertheless an immature fetus is considered to have life if it has only most recently been discharged, if it is white in color, and if it is without blotches or stains. In such a case it should be baptized at least conditionally.[53] Certain signs of death are advanced putrefaction or decomposition. In case of certain death baptism should not be administered, even conditionally.[54] The duty of determining these signs of death is incumbent on the physician; unless a skilled physician testifies that the apparently lifeless fetus is in reality without life, it should be baptized conditionally.[55] Doctors,

---

[49] Coronata, *De Sacramentis,* I, n. 126; Cappello, *De Sacramentis,* I, n. 159; Cenicot, *Institutiones Theologiae Moralis,* II, n. 141; Noldin-Schmitt, *Summa Theologiae Moralis,* I, n. 70; Capellmann, *Medicina Pastoralis,* p. 170.

[50] Cf. Vermeersch-Creusen, *Epitome Iuris Canonici,* II, n. 31; Vermeersch, *Theologia Moralis,* III, n. 239.

[51] Claeys Bouuaert-Simenon, *Manuale Juris Canonici,* II, n. 30.

[52] Genicot-Salsmans, *op. cit.,* II, n. 141.

[53] Coronata, *De Sacramentis,* I, n. 126.

[54] McAllister, *Emergency Baptism,* n. 40.

[55] Noldin-Schmitt, *Summa Theologia Moralis,* III, n. 70.

obstetricians, and even mothers should be warned not to omit baptism, even if signs of putrefaction are present. Since this may be only incipient putrefaction, it does not in any way furnish a completely reliable indication of certain death.[56] When death is not certain, so that one may question the absence of life in the fetus, precious time should not be lost through the making of any thorough examination for signs of life. Conditional baptism should immediately be conferred.[57]

A fetus which, when expelled about three months after conception, shows a human form should be baptized absolutely, if it is certainly living. If, however, a fetus is expelled before the completion of a three-month period after conception, or if it is conceived over three months but does not have a human form, it should be baptized conditionally. If doubt exists concerning the life of any fetus, no matter how long conceived, it should be baptized conditionally.[58]

In regard to the manner of baptism, this will, to a large extent, depend upon the size of the fetus and upon the prudently invoked decision of the physician or the nurse who may administer the sacrament. If the fetus is free of the membrane, it may be baptized by way of infusion, provided that warm water touches and flows on the fetus, preferably on the skin of the forehead.[59] To have greater assurance of the validity of the baptism, however, the safer and better method of baptizing the fetus is that of immersion. While the form of baptism is pronounced, the fetus should be immersed in warm water and then gradually withdrawn from it.[60] Moreover, Capellmann stated that when a fetus is six weeks old it is large enough to be capable of baptism by way of infusion, provided the membrane is removed from it. But he warned that such a method of procedure was not without risk, and therefore was not to be employed by persons not skilled in

---

[56] Cappello, *De Sacramentis,* I, n. 160.

[57] McFadden, *Medical Ethics,* p. 241.

[58] Merkelbach, *Summa Theologiae Moralis,* III, n. 158. Cf. canon 748.

[59] McAllister, *Emergency Baptism,* n. 40.

[60] Vermeersch-Creusen, *Epitome Iuris Canonici,* II, n. 31; Claeys Bouuaert-Simenon, *Manuale Juris Canonici,* II, n. 30.

this matter. In practice, unskilled persons should take the safest method by administering baptism through immersion, after the membranes of the fetus have been ruptured.[61] When urgent necessity will not allow for such delay as may be occasioned by the method of immersion, then the water should be poured over the whole exposed surface of the fetus.[62]

In the case of an expelled fetus or embryo which is enclosed in the membrane, there arises the question whether conditional baptism should first be administered on the membrane enveloping the fetus, and then be repeated on the fetus itself after the membrane is ruptured. This method, so Merkelbach (1871-1942) stated, should not be approved, for the membrane is not part of the fetus, and therefore the earlier act of baptizing would lack all possible validity.[63] There are those who claim that the exposure to the air will kill the fetus if the membrane is ruptured. But Capellmann claims the exposure to the air will not immediately destroy the life of the fetus, provided that the membrane is opened cautiously.[64] In practice, therefore, the membrane should always be ruptured, and the water of baptism should flow directly upon the fetus.

When the fetus is enclosed by the membrane, the safest method of ensuring the valid baptism of the fetus is to place the membranous fetus in warm water. "While the ovum is in the water and under the water, the membrane is ruptured, and immediately after the rupturing the conditional formula of baptism is pronounced: 'Si vivis, ego etc.' In order to rupture the membrane, the thumb and index finger of each hand should take hold of one of the folds of the envelope. When the membrane is ruptured, the whole contents of the ovum will flow out and will be washed by the baptismal water. This method also prevents exposure of the fetus to the air."[65]

---

[61] *Medicina Pastoralis,* p. 112.

[62] Bowen, *Baptism of the Infant and the Fetus,* p. 5.

[63] *Summa Theologiae Moralis,* III, n. 158.

[64] *Medicina Pastoralis,* p. 112.

[65] Capellmann, *loc. cit.;* this same method is approved by Cappello, *De Sacramentis,* I, n. 159; Coronata, *De Sacramentis,* I, n. 126; Lehmkuhl, *Theologia Moralis,* II, n. 103; Vermeersch-Creusen, *Epitome Iuris Canonici,* II, n. 31; Noldin-Schmitt, *Summa Theologiae Moralis,* III, n. 70; Claeys Bouuaert-Simenon, *Manuale Juris Canonici,* II, n. 30.

It should be the conscientious duty of every Catholic physician and nurse not to be too hasty in dismissing a mass of malformed flesh as not containing a fertilized ovum. Before making a final decision concerning a questionable mass, they should diligently explore its content.[66] If there is a reasonable foundation for doubting whether the ovum is animated with a rational soul, it should be baptized conditionally. On the other hand, however, if there is no reasonable foundation for such a doubt, in so far as it does not present even the first lineaments of a human body, it should not be baptized. The consultation of skilled physicians and the advice of a priest should be sought in particular cases.[67]

When a mother dies in pregnancy, there arises the obligation of extracting the fetus by means of an operation in order that it may be given baptism.[68] The source of this obligation is the grave precept of charity incumbent upon everyone to help his neighbor who may be placed in extreme spiritual necessity.[69] If there is hope that the infant is still alive, even though the mother is dead, there is a grave obligation on the part of physicians or surgeons to perform the operation. Prior to the fourth month, little hope can exist under such circumstances for extracting the child alive, and thus a grave obligation cannot be imposed.[70] When such an operation cannot be performed the fetus receives baptism *in utero.* There can be no existing grave obligation to perform the operation when it is morally certain that the fetus died either before the mother or with the mother, or when there is only the faintest hope of taking it alive from the mother.[71]

If the fourth month of gestation is completed, and especially if the mother suffered a sudden death, there generally is present

---

[66] Donovan, "What of This Baptismal Procedure in a State Hospital," *Homiletic and Pastoral Review,* XLIX (1948), 157.

[67] S. C. S. Off., 5 apr. 1713—*Collectanea S. Congregationis Propaganda Fide,* n. 282; *Fontes,* n. 777.

[68] Canon 746, § 4.

[69] Genicot, *Institutiones Theologiae Moralis,* II, n. 145; Noldin-Schmitt, *Summa Theologiae Moralis,* III, n. 70; Cappello, *De Sacramentis,* I, n. 158.

[70] Coronata, *De Sacramentis,* I, n. 125; Prümmer, *Manuale Theologiae Moralis,* III, n. 130.

[71] Genicot, *loc. cit.*

some hope of delivering the fetus alive.[72] Moreover, a physician should not be easily believed if, without making any special examination to discover the true facts in a particular case, he declares that the fetus has died, or that it cannot survive the completing of the operation to extract it.[73]

When there exists some hope that the fetus is still alive, it should be extracted as soon as possible. In the event it shows true signs of life, it should be baptized absolutely, but if only doubtful signs appear, it should be baptized conditionally.[74] Those who are competent to perform operations, namely surgeons and physicians, are bound by a grave obligation to extract the fetus immediately subsequent to the mother's death.[75] All precautions should be taken for the observance of the demand of the civil law in so far as it requires that only a certified physician should perform the operation, that competent witnesses give testimony of the woman's prior death, and that written permission for the performance of the operation be obtained from the woman's husband or relatives.[76] If the civil law permits it, then a nurse who is capable of performing this operation may extract the fetus in the absence of a surgeon or physician.[77]

Under no condition is the priest ever bound to perform such an operation. Even if he did not lack the needed skill to do so, the danger of scandal would always impend. The priest should not directly order that the operation be undertaken. The Christian sense of decency would require him to refuse to perform this operation, since it would not be proper to his vocation, and the act might well cause odious remarks to be made against the priesthood and the Church.[78] The Holy Office urged the missionaries in China especially to refrain from performing the operation

---

[72] Claeys Bouuaert-Simenon, *Manuale Juris Canonici,* II, n. 29.

[73] Lehmkuhl, *Theologia Moralis,* II, n. 104.

[74] Canon 746, § 4; Duffy, "Baptism in Cases of Difficult Parturition," *ER,* XLIX (1913), 613.

[75] Claeys Bouuaert-Simenon, *Manuale Juris Canonici,* II, n. 29.

[76] McAllister, *Emergency Baptism,* n. 38.

[77] McFadden, *Medical Ethics,* p. 244.

[78] Vermeersch-Creusen, *Epitome Iuris Canonici,* II, n. 30; Claeys Bouuaert-Simenon, *Manuale Juris Canonici,* II, n. 29.

themselves, and to commit the task of performing it to the physicians or surgeons.[79]

In the event, however, that the physician fails in his duty to perform the operation, or the husband or some relative fails to request it, then the duty of advising it rests upon the priest, and even of giving grave warnings to those concerned, since everything possible should be done to procure the eternal salvation of an immortal soul.[80] If a Catholic mother is dying in a Catholic hospital, the Sister in charge should immediately inform the physician of the fact and also make known to the relatives of the woman their grave duty of giving consent to the operation. In the event that the husband or relatives refuse to permit the operation, the obligation of the physician and the Sister ceases.[81] In order that the fetus may be baptized as soon as possible, the surgeon and relatives should be immediately notified, and everything required for both the operation and the administration of the sacrament should be placed near at hand.[82]

It is a grave obligation for chaplains of hospitals and for pastors in whose parishes a hospital is situated to warn physicians and obstetricians of their duty to ensure the baptism of an unborn infant or of an abortive fetus as soon as possible, when the infant or fetus may be in danger of death. In teaching or examining physicians on the principles involved, the priest should employ great prudence and caution, lest offense be given or ignorance be insinuated to these professional men, especially if they are non-Catholics. In addition to instructing physicians and nurses, the priest should impart in his prenuptial instructions the knowledge of the grave duty incumbent on parents, especially on the mother, to baptize a fetus in the event of a miscarriage.[83]

---

[79] S. C. S. Off., 15 febr. 1780—*Fontes,* n. 839; S. C. S. Off., 13 dec. 1899—*Collectanea S. Congregationis Propaganda Fide,* n. 2073.

[80] Vermeersch-Creusen, *loc. cit.;* McAllister, *Emergency Baptism,* n. 38.

[81] McAllister, *Emergency Baptism,* n. 38.

[82] McFadden, *Medical Ethics,* p. 245.

[83] Cappello, *De Sacramentis,* I, n. 160.

CHAPTER VI

The Church as the Proper Place of Solemn Baptism

Sect. I. The Parochial Church

In determining the suitable place for the administration of solemn baptism to either adults or infants, the Code has primarily decreed that the baptistery in a church or public oratory is the proper place for the conferring of the sacrament.[1] But the Code further qualifies the place of baptism by legislating that every parochial church should have a baptismal font,[2] and thus it directs that the baptismal font in the parochial church is the proper place for the licit administration of solemn baptism. This ecclesiastical law is in full harmony with the fact that the conferring of solemn baptism is among the functions reserved by the Code to the pastor.[3] Furthermore, the Code states that, although the priest is the ordinary minister of solemn baptism, yet its licit administration is the right of only the pastor, except in the case in which permission has been granted to another priest by the pastor or the local ordinary to administer the sacrament.[4]

A person's proper pastor becomes determined through the person's domicile or quasi-domicile as located within the territory of a particular parish.[5] To acquire a parochial domicile an adult would have to take up actual residence in some parish with the intention of remaining perpetually unless called away, or apart from such intention would need actually to have resided in a parish for ten complete years.[6] To acquire a parochial quasi-domicile an adult would have to take up actual residence in some parish with the intention of remaining for the greater part of the

[1] Canon 773.

[2] Canon 774, § 1.

[3] Canon 462, § 1.

[4] Canon 738, § 1.

[5] Canon 94, § 1.

[6] Canon 92, § 1.

year, or apart from such intention would need actually to have resided in a parish for the greater part of the year.[7] Thus the parochial church of a person to be baptized is the parochial church of the parish in which the person's domicile or quasi-domicile is located.

Since it is possible to have several domiciles simultaneously, or a domicile and a quasi-domicile concurrently, one may readily, as a consequence, look to several parishes for the element of legal pertinence and thus acknowledge, by reason of the multiplied domiciles and quasi-domiciles, several pastors with equal rights for the baptism.[8] An adult who has attained the year of his majority can select anyone of these parish churches as the proper place for the conferring of baptism upon him. This, however, is not the case with a minor, for he retains the domicile of the person to whom he is subject.[9] This constitutes his necessary or legal domicile. Consequently, the parochial church of the parish in which the domicile of his father or guardian is located is the proper place for the administering of solemn baptism to him.

In the case in which the father or guardian possesses also a quasi-domicile, Castello follows the opinion which denies that a minor can share in a legal quasi-domicile.[10] Nevertheless, he admits the solid probability of the opposite opinion, and thus in view of a *dubium iuris* it seems that the parochial church of the parish in which the father or guardian has a quasi-domicile may also be regarded as a proper place for the administration of solemn baptism to a minor. Accordingly the parochial churches of the parishes in which the domiciles or quasi-domiciles of the father or guardian are situated have equal rights, and the ultimate selection of a parochial church for the administering of solemn baptism to minors belongs to the father or guardian of the minor.

---

[7] Canon 92, § 2.

[8] Koudelka, *Pastors, Their Rights and Duties According to the New Code of Canon Law,* The Catholic University of America Canon Law Studies, n. 11 (Washington, D. C.: The Catholic University of America, 1921), p. 73.

[9] Canon 93, § 1.

[10] Costello, *Domicile and Quasi-Domicile,* The Catholic University of American Canon Law Studies, n. 60 (Washington, D. C.: The Catholic University of America, 1930), p. 177.

In the case of an adult, whether in his majority or in his minority,[11] the Code does not give his parish church the preference as the proper place for the conferring of solemn baptism. Rather, ecclesiastical law states that solemn baptism in this case, when it can be suitably arranged, should be conferred by the ordinary or his delegate.[12] Moreover, it further directs that the solemn baptism of adult converts should be conferred, if it can be conveniently done, in the cathedral on the vigils of Easter and Pentecost.[13] This law is, however, not of strict obligation; its implementation depends on the option of the bishop, who may either conform to it, or decline from it. In the usual case in which the bishop foregoes his right as granted him by the Code it cannot be said that he dispenses from the law; rather, he simply makes use of his freedom to accept or decline the exercise of his right. This reservation is not customary in this country,[14] and thus bishops do not oblige pastors to make any report to the chancery concerning the forthcoming baptism of an adult. When the ordinary declines his right to baptize a convert in the cathedral, then the right to confer the sacrament devolves upon the pastor of the church which serves the territory in which the catechumen has a domicile or a quasi-domicile.

In the United States it has been the practice to permit the pastor or the priest who instructed the convert to administer the baptism in the parochial church to which he is attached, though this church be not the proper parochial church of the catechumen. Such a permission is not in any way conceded by the common law. This permission derives from the immemorial custom which exists in the United States to the effect that the priest who instructed the convert may also baptize him in a parochial church other than that which is located within the confines of the proper

[11] Canon 745, § 2, 2°.—Adulti autem censentur, qui rationis usu fruuntur; idque satis est ut suo quisque animi motu baptismum petat et ad illum admittatur.

[12] Canon 744.

[13] Canon 772.

[14] Augustine, *A Commentary on the New Code of Canon Law,* IV, 45.

parish of the catechumen.[15] By reason of this immemorial custom a convert may receive his baptism in a parochial church to which he does not belong, for the continuance of this custom may be tolerated by the local ordinary when he judges that it cannot prudently be set aside in the face of particular personal or local circumstances.[16] In the absence of this immemorial custom, the ordinary could likewise concede permission by statute or by special delegation for the baptizing of a convert in a parochial church not located within the territory of the proper parish of the catechumen.[17]

Before the promulgation of the Code it was not required that a baptismal font be erected in every parochial church, for in some districts only the cathedral or a few parochial churches enjoyed the prerogative of maintaining a font for the conferring of solemn baptism. As a consequence the baptismal font was not an essential part of the parochial church.[18] But the present ecclesiastical law ordains and prescribes that every parochial church must possess a baptismal font, no matter how extended or restricted the parish may be, and no matter how long it has been established.

In the case of a division of a parish and the formation of one or more new parishes it is forbidden by the common law that there be reserved to the mother church any exclusive right for the administering of the sacrament of baptism. Each new parochial church has a right to possess a baptismal font.[19]

As a further precaution against the revival of this pristine situation which did not permit every parochial church to have a baptismal font, the Code has expressly reprobated every statute, privilege or custom contrary to this law.[20] Since, therefore, such a former contrary custom is expressly reprobated, it is considered a corruption relative to the present legislation, even though its

---

[15] "National Parishes: Affiliation and Separation," *ER,* LXXXVII (1932), 531.

[16] Canon 5.

[17] Waldron, *The Minister of Baptism,* p. 87.

[18] Claeys Bouuaert-Simenon, *Manuale Juris Canonici,* II, n. 52.

[19] Canon 1427, § 4.

[20] Canon 774, § 1.

existence has stood immemorial. Under such circumstances the present law absolutely prohibits the revival of such a custom in the future.[21] Besides, even if this contrary custom were again in existence for the ordinary period of time as prescribed in the law,[22] yet the additional element of reasonableness as required for the introducing a custom contrary to the law would be lacking. For the law definitely states that a custom which is expressly reprobated is not reasonable,[23] and it is precisely the element of unreasonableness inherent in customs arising counter or contrary to the law that renders them absolutely and perpetually void of any counter-effects; in addition to the reprobation of any contrary custom, also any contrary statute is permanently outlawed, regardless of its particular or other legitimate character.[24] Finally, any privilege permitting this former practice is reprobated. The law here explicitly intervenes against the application of the ruling as contained in canon 4, which allows it as a rule that there remain in force all privileges conceded by the Holy See previously to the Code, in the event, of course, that they were still in use at the time of the promulgation of the Code. Thus the reprobation contained in canon 74 is of such a nature as to make impossible in the future the establishment of any statute or custom which would forbid a parochial church to possess or make use of a baptismal font.[25]

In prescribing that every parochial church should possess a baptismal font, the Code at the same time points to the baptistery as the proper location for the baptismal font in the parochial church.[26] Nevertheless, even though the Code explicitly indicates that the administration of the sacrament should take place in a baptistery, ecclesiastical law does not as much insist on the fact that every parochial church have a baptistery as it urges that every parish church should at least possess a baptismal font. Ec-

---

[21] Canon 5.

[22] Canon 27, § 2.

[23] Canon 27, § 2.

[24] Blat, *Commentarium,* Lib. III, Pars I, tit. I, n. 64.

[25] De Clercq, *Traité de Droit Canonique,* II, n. 57.

[26] Canon 773.

clesiastical law considers it fitting and proper for every parish church to possess a baptistery, but the law makes it obligatory for every parochial church to erect a baptismal font.

The baptistery is that part of the church within which is enclosed the baptismal font that serves for baptism. Whenever it is possible, there should be a separate chapel, located off the nave of the church, and, if the chapel be large enough, it should also contain an altar.[27] When a separate chapel is not possible, the baptistery should at least be railed off, or else a screen or similar separation should mark it off from the nave floor. The gate leading into the baptistery should be locked when the font is not in use, and the floor of the baptistery should be at least one step below the level of the church floor. So much importance is attached to the baptistery that it is considered second in rank after the high altar as a sacred part of the church.[28]

Although ecclesiastical law does not determine the exact location in the church for the baptismal font,[29] the *Roman Ritual* decrees that it should be placed within a screened enclosure, and should be constructed of substantial material which can serve for the storing of water. Besides, it should be sealed under lock and key, should be of becoming shape and ornamentation, and should be so covered that dust or any other unclean substance is precluded from all possible penetration.[30] The baptismal font should be made of marble or of stone. It can also be made of wood or of metal, but, if it is made of wood, then the interior of the font must be lined with metal.[31] The Sacred Congregation for the Propagation

---

[27] Weber, "The Baptistery and Font," *The Homiletic and Pastoral Review,* XXVII (1927), 1288.

[28] Attwater, *A Catholic Dictionary* (12th printing, New York: The Macmillan Company, 1945), p. 50.

[29] Woywod, "Place of Baptistery," *Homiletic and Pastoral Review,* XXXVIII (1937-1938), 632.

[30] Tit. II, cap. I, n. 46; Aertnys, *Compendium Liturgiae Sacrae* (11. ed., Romae: Domus Editorialis Marietti, Sanctae Sedis Apostolicae et Sacrae *Rituum Congregationis Typographi,* 1943), n. 221.

[31] Moretti, *De Sacris Functionibus Episcopo Celebrante, assistante, Absente* (4 vols., Taurini: Marietti, 1936-1939), I, n. 170 (hereafter cited *De Sacris Functionibus*).

of the Faith decreed that, when baptismal fonts cannot be made of marble, they may instead be made of brick.[32] In the basin of the font there should be two compartments, the one containing the baptismal water, and the other serving for the receiving of the water poured over the head of the child, and containing a drain for conducting the used water to the sacrarium in the ground.[33] As regards the cover, it should be made of wood or metal, and should be arranged so that it can easily be moved. It should be suitably ornamented, preferably with the image of St. John the Baptist baptizing Christ, unless perchance this image is already depicted in a mural in the baptistery. A white canopy should be placed over the whole cover. When the baptismal font is not located in a special chapel or baptistery, then an iron rail should be placed around the font, and the gate attached to it should be securely locked when the font is not being used.[34]

In accord with the *Roman Ritual* the baptismal font must be blessed on Holy Saturday and on the Vigil of Pentecost.[35] Now, the Code indeed states that the blessing of the baptismal font on Holy Saturday is one of the duties reserved to the pastor,[36] but it makes no mention of the Vigil of Pentecost. Nevertheless, the blessing of the font on the Vigil of Pentecost is just as obligatory on the pastor as is the blessing of it on Holy Saturday. If the Code decrees nothing new concerning the rites and ceremonies which are prescribed in the liturgical books approved by the Church for the administration of the sacraments and sacramentals, then all liturgical laws extant previous to the promulgation of the Code remain unchanged.[37] Since the *Roman Ritual* prescribes the blessing of the font on the Vigil of Pentecost as well as on Holy Saturday, and since the Code has not expressly abrogated

---

[32] S. C. de Prop. Fide, 14 mart. 1922—Bouscaren, *Canon Law Digest* (2 vols. and *Supplement through 1948,* Milwaukee: The Bruce Publishing Company, 1934-1949), II, 446, ad 3.

[33] "Baptismal Font," *The Catholic Encyclopedia* (15 vols., with Index and 2 Supplements, New York, 1907-1922), II, 275.

[34] Moretti, *De Sacris Functionibus,* I, n. 170.

[35] Tit. II, cap. I, n. 4.

[36] Canon 462, § 7.

[37] Canon 2.

this law, it must be concluded that the blessing of the font on the Eve of Pentecost is an obligatory ritual function incumbent on the pastor. Moreover, in recent times the Holy See has made it evident that the single blessing of the font on Holy Saturday is not in compliance with ecclesiastical law. When the Diocese of Cremona, Italy, requested the Holy See to approve the custom of blessing the font only once a year, on Holy Saturday, the Holy See replied that the font is to be blessed in all parish churches both on Holy Saturday and on the Vigil of Pentecost.[38] For a just cause, however, a dispensation may be obtained from the blessing on one or the other of these two days.[39]

By reason of the fact that every parish church must possess a baptismal font,[40] it follows that every pastor must conduct the function of blessing the font in his parochial church. It is not admissible to limit the blessing of the font to the mother church.[41] If, perchance, there are other churches besides the parochial church which have fonts within the confines of the parish, the pastor of the parochial church may depute other priests to conduct the ceremonies of blessing their fonts on Holy Saturday and on the Vigil of Pentecost.[42]

When because of unavoidable circumstances the new oils blessed by the bishop have not arrived in time for the ceremony on Holy Saturday, then the priest blesses the font, but omits the adding of the holy oils. After the new oils have come, he adds them privately with the prayers given in the *Missal.* But if baptism must be administered before the arrival of the new oils, the pastor uses the old oils. In this case, even if the new oils arrive soon after Holy Saturday, nevertheless the priest does not bless new water and add the new oils until the Vigil of Pentecost.[43] If for some

---

[38] S. C. C., *Resolutio, Cremonen.,* 10 iun. 1922—*AAS,* XV (1923), 225.

[39] Cf. S. R. C., 7 iun. 1892—*Fontes,* n. 6215. Found in *Il Monitore Ecclesiastico,* Serie 4, Vol. V (1923), 205.

[40] Canon 774, § 1.

[41] Coronata, *De Sacramentis,* I, n. 154; S. C. R., 13 ian. 1899, ad I—*Fontes,* n. 6287.

[42] S. C. R., 13 ian. 1899, ad 4—*Fontes,* n. 6287.

[43] S. C. R., 23 sept. 1837, ad 3—*Fontes,* n. 5893.

reason the holy oils cannot be blessed in a particular year, as may happen in time of war, pestilence or persecution, then the oils blessed in the previous year may be used in the blessing of the font. The baptismal water already at hand should not be poured into the sacrarium upon the arrival of the new oils.[44] If only one or two baptisms occur in a rural parochial church between Easter and Pentecost, and if there be a scarcity of oil and chrism, then O'Kane suggested that the celebrant make the sign of the cross on the surface of the water with his thumb or with an instrument of silver, after he has dipped either one of them in the oilstocks.[45]

It is never permitted to bless baptismal water on Holy Saturday or on the Vigil of Pentecost with the shorter formula contained in the *Roman Ritual,* for this formula is to be used only in cases of necessity. When the ceremonies according to the *Missal* cannot be carried out, then the ceremonies according to the formula of the *Small Ritual* of Benedict XIII (1724-1730) are to be observed. In the event that not even these ceremonies of the blessing of the font can be performed, then it is better to omit the blessing of the font entirely on Holy Saturday and on the Vigil of Pentecost.[46]

In a parish where a baptismal font will be lacking for some peculiar reason, the pastor must omit the blessing of the baptismal water. In such a case he is obliged to bless baptismal water only when his supply has become putrid or has been exhausted. In blessing baptismal water in these circumstances he can make use of a short formula, which was conceded by Pope Paul III (1534-1549) to the missionaries of Peru and the Indies, and which was extended to the United States at the petition of the I Provincial Council of Baltimore (1829) by Pope Pius VIII (1829-1830).[47]

---

[44] S. C. R., 23 sept. 1837, ad 1—*Fontes,* n. 5893.

[45] *Notes on the Rubrics of the Roman Ritual,* n. 556; "Consecrating the Font at Pentecost in Rural Parishes," *ER,* LII (1915), 93.

[46] Woywod, "Blessing of Baptismal Water," *Homiletic and Pastoral Review,* XXIII (1923), 749.

[47] "Blessing Baptismal Water in a Church without a Font," *ER,* XCVI (1937), 188. Cf. *Coll. Lac.,* III, 33-34.

SECT. II. THE NON-PAROCHIAL CHURCH WITH A FONT

By a non-parochial church, one may understand a church that does not serve the specific needs of a parish, or does not serve as a capitular church, or does not serve for a religious community, as a church attached to the religious house.[48] Again, a non-parochial church may indeed serve as a capitular church or as a church annexed to a connected religious house, but still may exist as a church with which there is not connected the care of souls. Since no distinction is made in canon 773 between the different kinds of churches, and since canon 774, § 2, treats concerning non-parochial churches without any distinction, a baptistery or baptismal font can, under certain required conditions, be erected in all these non-parochial churches. Primarily, it is required that these non-parochial churches possess the canonical status of a church.[49]

In addition to the non-parochial church, any chapel the status of which is that of a public oratory[50] may under certain conditions likewise possess the habitual right of a baptistery or a baptismal font. But this right of erecting a baptistery or a baptismal font is limited to only a church or a public oratory.[51] The Code states in two canons that a baptismal font may be placed in a public oratory, and thus clearly implies that this right cannot be possessed by a semi-public[52] or by a private oratory.[53]

Coronata expressly states that, since the ordinary may withdraw a sacred place from the jurisdiction of a pastor, he may concede the permission of erecting a baptismal font in a semi-public oratory when a just cause exists.[54] Mothon is of the opinion that a semi-public oratory is clearly implied in the Code when it permits public oratories to possess baptismal fonts, because in such a case the term is used to distinguish all other oratories

---

[48] Canon 479, § 1.

[49] Canon 1161.

[50] Canon 1188, § 2, 1°.

[51] Canon 773.

[52] Canon 1188, § 2, 2°.

[53] Canon 1188, § 2, 3°.

[54] *De Sacramentis,* I, n. 154.

from private oratories.[55] Despite the fact that these two authors maintain these opinions, there nevertheless seems to be no foundation for such a deduction in the texts of the canons of the Code. Hence, the words of the Code permit to a public oratory the legitimate possession of a baptismal font,[56] and neither explicitly nor implicitly extend this permission to semi-public oratories, even if these oratories are blessed.[57]

If, by reason of a statute, privilege or custom, a church before the promulgation of the Code possessed an exclusive right to administer baptism to all who lived in a certain city, town or district, it no longer can maintain this right to the exclusion of the rights of the parochial churches in the district. The Code now obliges every parochial church to possess a baptismal font.[58] Since the promulgation of the Code, these non-parochial churches do not indeed forfeit their former right of conferring baptism to those who live within the confines of a certain district, but their right has now become a cumulative right with the rights of the parochial churches. The cumulative right to a font is the right whereby the recipients may lawfully seek baptism at such a font as well as in their own parish churches.[59] Even if new parishes are created within the district, these newly erected parochial churches still have to share their right of baptizing their parishioners with the non-parochial church which possesses a cumulative right over all who live within the same parochial area. As a consequence, these non-parochial churches may administer baptism to persons from any of those parishes where in former times they had the exclusive right of baptism and also to parishioners from new parishes within the same determined district. In conjunction with this right of the non-parochial church, however,

---

[55] *Institutions Canoniques,* II, art. 1696 and 1698.

[56] Feldhaus, *Oratories,* The Catholic University of America Canon Law Studies, n. 42 (Washington, D. C.: The Catholic University of America, 1927), p. 97.

[57] Augustine, *Commentary on the New Code of Canon Law,* IV, 88; Blat, *Commentarium*—see p. 84, lib. III, pars I, n. 65; Ayrinhac, *Legislation on the Sacraments,* p. 58; Aertnys-Damen, *Theologia Moralis,* II, n. 78.

[58] Canon 774, § 1.

[59] Blat, *op. cit.,* lib. II, Pars I, n. 64.

each parish church possesses the right to baptize its own subjects when they come to it.[60]

This institution exists in Rome, where a number of infants from the parishes of Rome are brought to St. Peter's Basilica for the reception of baptism, and in Florence, where infants are frequently brought to the baptistery of St. John. In fact, St. Peter's Basilica possesses a cumulative right with all parish churches throughout the world, so that it can administer baptism to persons from all parts of the globe.[61]

If a non-parochial church has a cumulative right, it is not required that the permission of the proper pastor be obtained either by the parent or the person seeking baptism or by the rector of the non-parochial church. By reason of this right all baptisms are licit which are conferred on those who have a domicile or quasi-domicile within the definitely established district. The obligation, however, is incumbent on the rector of this non-parochial church to inform the proper pastor as soon as possible of the administration of baptism to one of his parishioners, in order that he may inscribe this fact in the baptismal record.[62] The cumulative right, where it is legitimately possessed, is limited exclusively to the administration of the sacrament of baptism. As a consequence, any church which can establish this right cannot vindicate the same right with parish churches in other parochial functions.[63]

After the promulgation of the Code this cumulative right cannot be acquired through the agency of usage or custom. A response of the Commission for the Interpretation of the Code prohibits the introduction of such a cumulative right through such a means.[64] Such a custom would be regarded as a corruption or an abuse of the law, and thus it is expressly reprobated and is, therefore, not reasonable.[65] When a custom is not reasonable, it cannot become a

[60] Coronata, *De Sacramentis,* I, n. 154.

[61] Fanfani, *De Iure Parochorum,* n. 233.

[62] Woywod, *A Practical Commentary on the Code of Canon Law,* I, n. 671.

[63] Beste, *Introductio in Codicem* (3. ed., Collegeville, Minn.: St. John's Abbey Press, 1946), p. 488.

[64] Commissio Pontificia Interpretationis (C. P. I.), 12 nov. 1922, IV—*AAS,* XIV (1922), 662. Found in Bouscaren, *Canon Law Digest,* I, 345.

[65] Canon 27, § 2.

law.[66] If before the promulgation of the Code the cumulative right was introduced through custom, the ordinary can for a reason of prudence tolerate this preexisting custom,[67] or he may also permit it to continue if it was founded on an acquired right which has not been expressly revoked by the Code.[68]

Aside from custom, however, the ordinary may permit or order that a baptismal font be placed in a non-parochial church or in a public oratory within the confines of a parish.[69] This church or public oratory can then enjoy a right with the parish church in the administration of baptism. The erection of this baptismal font in the church or public oratory is dependent on either a permission conceded by the ordinary at the request of the faithful or of the pastor, or else on the mandate of the bishop. Though it is not absolutely necessary, this permission should be expressed. It is not the prerogative of the pastor but only of the bishop to concede the permission. In the case of the mandate, it seeks for its purpose to obtain some good for the faithful, and the refusal of the pastor will not void it.[70] The cause for granting this concession will generally be either such a factor as the great distance which the people of the parish will have to travel to reach the parochial church, or else some serious difficulty which the people experience in reaching it, either because of bad roads or because of poor transportation systems. This concession is especially warranted in missionary territory, and is convenient for missionary stations or missions attached to a more centrally located church.[71]

It is not the right of the rector or the priest who administers this church or public oratory in which the baptismal font is situated to confer the solemn baptism.[72] Rather, it is the right of the pastor of the parish within which this church or public oratory is located to administer the solemn baptism in these places for the accommo-

---

[66] Canon 27, § 1.

[67] Canon 5.

[68] Canon 4.

[69] Canon 774, § 2.

[70] Claeys Bouuaert-Simenon, *Manuale Juris Canonici,* II, n. 52.

[71] Augustine, *A Commentary on the New Code of Canon Law,* IV, 90.

[72] De Clercq, *Traité de Droit Canonique,* II, n. 57.

dation of the faithful, or else of some other priest whom the pastor has delegated for the exercise of this right.[73] The rector of this non-parochial church or the chaplain of the public oratory may licitly administer the sacrament only with the permission of the proper pastor of the parish in which the church or the public oratory is located. Thus the pastor has the right to administer baptism not only in his parish church, but also in those churches or oratories which are located within the confines of his parish and possess a baptismal font.

Despite the fact that a parent who presents his child for baptism, or a convert who seeks baptism, may sometimes have a double choice in regard to the place for the reception of baptism, still the selection of a church other than the parochial church does not change the recipient's affiliation with his proper parish. In the case of a child he becomes a member of the parish in which the father or the guardian has a domicile at the time of his baptism, and in the case of a convert he immediately becomes a parishioner of that parish in which he has a domicile or quasi-domicile.

In regard to the blessing of the baptismal font on Holy Saturday and on the Vigil of Pentecost in those non-parochial churches or public oratories which possess a fixed font, the Sacred Congregation of Rites directed that it was admissible for these churches or oratories to conduct this sacred function, even though a similar service was conducted in the parish church.[74] When it is not possible to perform the entire blessing in the non-parochial church because there is an insufficient supply of holy oils for both the parochial and non-parochial churches, then enough baptismal water should be blessed in the parish church for some of it to be taken to the church or the public oratory which within the boundaries of the parish has a fixed font.[75]

---

[73] Canon 738, § 1.

[74] S. R. C., *Mantuana,* 1 mart. 1636—*Decreta Authentica Congregationis Sacrorum Rituum ex actis eiusdem Collecta eiusque Auctoritate promulgata sub Auspiciis SS. Domini nostri Leonis Papae XIII* (5 vols. et 2 Appendices, Romae: Ex Typographia Polyglotta, 1898-1927), n. 630. (Hereafter referred to as the *Decreta Authentica Congregationis Sacrorum Rituum.*)

[75] S. R. C., 29 maii, 1900, ad 1—*Fontes*, n. 6305.

Although the blessing of the font should be conducted in the parish church on Holy Saturday and on the Vigil of Pentecost, yet it is not absolutely obligatory on non-parochial churches and public oratories which possess a font.[76] As a consequence, the practice on the part of such non-parochial churches to receive baptismal water from the parish church for putting it in the baptismal font can be considered lawful.[77]

SECT. III. THE NON-PAROCHIAL CHURCH WITHOUT A FONT

When on account of special circumstances a person cannot come to the parochial church, or to some other church or public oratory which enjoys the right of possessing a baptismal font, without incurring some inconvenience or danger, then the pastor should confer baptism in the closest church or public oratory which is within the confines of the parish.[78] Such a serious inconvenience will generally arise from the factor of distance. Ecclesiastical law in no way requires a determined measure of distance before the pastor can avail himself of the right, granted to him by the Code, to permit the administration of baptism in a non-parochial church which has no baptismal font. In this case the measure of distance exists entirely and essentially as a relative norm. Other factors may make a comparatively short distance a source of grave inconvenience. Bad roads, roads through a mountainous terrain, and roads covered with ice and snow for a rather long period of time may easily warrant the concession of this permission. Moreover, stormy or extremely cold weather could easily contribute to making travel a grave hardship. Again, the unavailability of transportation may prevent a person from going to the parish church, or the expense of traveling a considerable distance may impose a serious inconvenience on a poor family.

Difficulties in this regard may arise from other factors besides distance, as may happen when a contagious disease is prevalent and special precautions must be exercised. Moreover, travel may

---

[76] Coronata, *De Sacramentis,* I, n. 154; S. C. de Prop. Fide, 11 sept. 1779, ad 5—*Collectanea Sacrae Congregationis de Propaganda Fide,* n. 537.

[77] Augustine, *Commentary on the New Code of Canon Law,* IV, 90.

[78] Canon 775.

be dangerous during the time of war, or even when there exists for anyone who travels the threat of being seized by roaming bandits, as may be the case in some missionary lands. The consideration of inconvenience is not confined solely to the infant or the person who is to be baptized, but has applicable reference also to the parents or the godparents, who may be in bad health or who may have other physical weaknesses.[79] It is postulated, however, that no opportunity be given for the ceasing of this inconvenience within a short time, perhaps of about a week's duration.[80]

The concession of this permission is not the exclusive prerogative of the ordinary, for the pastor is not in any way required either to seek the ordinary's permission or to notify him of the exercise of the right. For the lawful concession of this permission all that is required is that some danger or grave inconvenience exists for the person to be baptized, for the parents, the guardians or the godparents. In this case the judgment concerning the danger or inconvenience is not reserved to the bishop, but to the pastor. If, however, the pastor is accustomed to grant this permission freely without fully weighing the true facts concerning the existence of a grave danger or inconvenience, the ordinary of the place has the right to reserve the judgment to himself because of such manifest laxity.[81]

In conceding permission for the administration of baptism in a non-parochial church without a font, the pastor of the parish within the confines of which the church or oratory is located should always ask the consent of the rector or the chaplain in charge of the place of worship. Under certain circumstances, especially if the rector or the chaplain readily consents to the use of the church or the oratory, the pastor may presume the consent of the priest in charge to baptize there. If the rector or the chaplain refuses without a just cause, then the pastor may have recourse to the ordinary. In cases, however, of urgent necessity in which immediate recourse cannot be had to the ordinary, the pastor may ignore the refusal

[79] Blat, *Commentarium,* lib. III, pars I, n. 65.

[80] Claeys Bouuaert-Simenon, *Manuale Juris Canonici,* II, n. 52.

[81] Coronata, *De Sacramentis,* I, n. 154.

of the rector or the chaplain and may proceed to baptize in such a church or oratory.[82]

If, perchance, the person to be baptized has easy access to a church or oratory in another parish, but would find as much difficulty in going to a non-parochial church within the confines of his own parish as to his own parish church, then there seems to be no reason for a pastor to refuse permission for his baptism in a non-parochial church outside the limits of the parish. Under such conditions it would seem more in keeping with the law to permit the administration of baptism to a parishioner in a non-parochial church outside the parish than to grant permission for baptism in the home of the person. The law prefers that the sacrament be conferred in a church or a public oratory.[83] Moreover the law does permit the administration of baptism to a person in a parish other than his own, and by the pastor of that parish, when danger of delay or some serious difficulty prevents the person from being baptized in his own parish and by his proper pastor.[84]

Although this non-parochial church has no baptismal font, nevertheless baptismal water should always be used in the administration of baptism.[85] Moreover, since the church or oratory has no baptismal font, the blessing of baptismal water should be omitted on Holy Saturday and on the Vigil of Pentecost. Consequently, when the pastor of the parish concedes permission for the administration of baptism in a non-parochial church or oratory without a font, the baptismal water should be obtained from the parish church, unless such a procedure become impossible or gravely inconvenient.

SCHOLION. SOLEMN BAPTISM IN HOSPITAL CHAPELS

The consideration here given to the administration of solemn baptism in hospital chapels abstracts completely from private baptism given in cases of necessity. Private baptism in hospitals will indeed be the more general occurrence, while solemn baptism

---

[82] De Clercq, *Traité de Droit Canonique,* II, n. 58.

[83] Canon 773.

[84] Canon 738, § 2.

[85] Fanfani, *De Iure Parochorum,* n. 239.

will be the exception. Occasionally, however, there does arise a situation which is not an emergency, and which will not admit, therefore, of the administration of private baptism. Nevertheless, the situation seems grave enough to warrant the administration of solemn baptism in the hospital chapel, so that it would hardly tolerate a prolonged delay in the administration of the sacrament, for baptism is indeed to be administered *quamprimum.*[86]

Although the ordinary minister of solemn baptism is a priest, ecclesiastical law reserves its licit administration to the proper pastor or local ordinary of the person to be baptized.[87] Since in the majority of cases the patients in a hospital are not the subjects of the pastor of the parish in which the hospital is situated, the local pastor cannot licitly administer solemn baptism to these non-subjects, except with the permission of their proper pastor or ordinary as their agent. The practice of priests to accept for baptism children who belonged to another parish to which they could easily have been brought without delay was condemned by the II Plenary Council of Baltimore (1866) as a very serious abuse.[88]

A patient outside his parochial territory in a hospital, whether he is an infant or an adult, is to be considered a *peregrinus,* but he is still subject to his proper pastor. If, however, he cannot easily and without delay return to his local parish church to be baptized, the Church's law makes an exception in such a case.[89] When either one of these factors is present, namely unavoidable inconvenience or undue delay in reaching the proper parish church, then such a person may receive baptism from the local pastor, since the duty of approaching the proper pastor no longer exists.[90] This may very well be the case when an infant cannot be taken out of the hospital for several weeks after his birth because he needs the special care and vigilance of the doctors and nurses. He is not in a danger of death, and as a consequence he cannot receive private baptism. But if baptism is delayed until he can be brought to his parish church,

---

[86] Canon 770.

[87] Canon 738, § 1; Drumm, *Hospital Chaplains,* p. 112.

[88] II Plenary Council of Baltimore (1866), *Acta et Decreta,* n. 227.

[89] Canon 738, § 2.

[90] Waldron, "Hospital Baptisms," *The Jurist* (Washington, D. C., 1941—), III (1943), 587-594.

the law of the Code requiring the administration of baptism *quamprimum* will not be observed, and, moreover, the child will be exposed for a longer period of time to the possible danger of dying without baptism. Hence, if a child is going to remain in the hospital for a period of over three or four weeks, it seems that this delay will warrant his reception of solemn baptism in that institution.

In some cases, under the conditions indicated later on in this discussion, the right of baptizing in a hospital an infant or an adult patient who cannot be brought to his proper parish without inconvenience and delay will belong, not to the local pastor, but to the chaplain of the institution. With respect to a chaplain's appointments, it may be so arranged that he may baptize solemnly without infringing on the right of the local pastor. This would be the case if the chaplain is appointed *simpliciter* without any specification concerning his powers as chaplain, but with the determination that he is constituted a *vicarius cooperator ad hoc* of the pastor of the parish in which the hospital is situated.[91] Again, though a hospital is not exempt by law, for a just and grave cause it can be withdrawn from the jurisdiction of the local pastor by the local ordinary.[92] In such a case the chaplain of the hospital would be appointed with the status of a pastor *pleno iure,* and would maintain a parochial jurisdiction over all who resided in the institution. Finally, the chaplain of the hospital could be appointed as a delegate of the ordinary with full pastoral powers. Under such circumstances he would exercise a pastoral jurisdiction which would be delegated and not ordinary.[93]

In addition to establishing the right of the local pastor or chaplain of the hospital to administer solemn baptism to *peregrini* when they cannot easily and without delay be brought to their proper parochial church, there arises the question of whether a hospital chapel is the proper and lawful place for the conferring of this sacrament. Ecclesiastical law directs that solemn baptism should be conferred in the baptistery of a church or a public oratory.[94] Now, a hos-

---

[91] Waldron, *The Minister of Baptism,* p. 114.

[92] Canon 464, § 2.

[93] Waldron, *op. cit.,* p. 115.

[94] Canon 773.

pital chapel is normally a semipublic oratory, since it is erected for the accommodation not of all the faithful, but of a community or group of people.[95] Moreover, a decree of the Sacred Congregation of Rites explicitly listed among the different kinds of semipublic oratories the oratory attached to a hospital.[96] As a consequence, it must be maintained that the mind of the legislator favors the erection of hospital chapels as semipublic oratories. It may happen occasionally, however, that a local ordinary has erected a public oratory in a hospital. This, however, would be an exceptional case, and will be determined from the document of erection, issued under the authority of the local ordinary.[97] Unless there is positive proof in the form of such a document, a hospital chapel is to be considered a semipublic oratory.

Inasmuch, then, as hospital chapels are semipublic oratories, it must be inferred from the Church's law that solemn baptism cannot be licitly administered in them.[98] A local ordinary is not authorized to erect a baptismal font in a hospital chapel, since the Church's law permits him to do so only in a church or a public oratory.[99] As a consequence, the practical solution under circumstances which frequently pave the way for the administration of solemn baptism in a particular hospital in which the chapel is a semipublic oratory is that the ordinary apply to the Holy See for an indult conceding the erection of a baptismal font in the oratory of this institution. On the other hand, if the occasions that give rise to the conferring of solemn baptism in a hospital chapel are infrequent, then the permission of the ordinary should be sought in each case. When a just and reasonable cause exists, the law of the Code gives the right to the ordinary to permit the administration of solemn baptism in a private oratory or at home in single extraordinary instances.[100] It should be reasoned *a fortiori* that the ordinary can grant a similar permission under the same circumstances for the administration of solemn baptism in the semipublic

---

[95] Canon 1188, § 2, 2°.

[96] S. R. C., decr. 23 ian. 1899—*Fontes,* n. 6288.

[97] Canon 1191, § 1.

[98] Canon 773.

[99] Canon 774, § 2.

[100] Canon 776, § 1, 2°.

oratory of a hospital. Certainly, the detention of an infant in the hospital for three or four weeks would be a just and reasonable cause for the conferring of solemn baptism in the hospital chapel.

Thus the local pastor or the chaplain of the hospital, upon whomsoever devolves the right of baptizing the *peregrini* when they cannot easily and without delay be brought to their parochial church, should apply to the local ordinary for permission to administer solemn baptism in a hospital chapel, unless the ordinary has already by means of an indult erected a baptismal font in the chapel. In addition, the local pastor of the hospital or its chaplain who has full pastoral powers should also obtain the permission of the proper pastor of the infant or adult who is to be baptized.

Should the chapel ot a hospital have the status of a public oratory, then the ordinary can for the accommodation of the residents of the institution permit or direct that a baptismal font be erected in it. In the absence of the baptismal font, however, the local pastor of the hospital or the chaplain of the institution who possesses full pastoral power can confer solemn baptism in such a public oratory, when its residents cannot without grave inconvenience, danger or delay be brought to their proper parish church.[101]

---

[101] Canon 775.

CHAPTER VII

Solemn Baptism Outside the Church or Oratory

SECT. I. IN PRIVATE HOUSES UPON LEGITIMATE REQUEST

Although ecclesiastical law decrees that the proper place for the licit administration of solemn baptism is the baptistery in a church or a public oratory,[1] nevertheless the Code permits an exception to this common norm under special circumstances. Among the occasions warranting an exception to the common norm, the Code lists the conferring of baptism on the children or the grandchildren of the highest acting ruler of a nation.[2] In such cases solemn baptism may be administered at home if it is properly requested by the ruler or by his children, when these are already adults as regards the reception of baptism.[3] Moreover, the Code extends this exception even to the children and grandchildren of him who is the prospective successor to the highest ruler of a country.

Who is comprehended by the Code as the highest ruler of a country? First of all it must be clearly understood that such a ruler need not be of royal blood and possess the royal title of king, emperor or prince. When the Code uses the word *throne* in canon 776, § 1, 1°, it does not intend the word to be taken in a restricted sense, but in a broad sense,[4] so that it embraces the principal leader of any government. Thus he may function under the title of president, premier, governor or of any other title which designates the head of a republic or a state. For this reason not only the president of a country, but a governor of one of the states, such as exists in the United States, can be included under the general phrase of the Code.[5] Such a ruler must be a legitimate head of the state, and any ruler who has unlawfully usurped the throne or principal govern-

[1] Canon 773.

[2] Canon 776, § 1, 1°

[3] Canon 745, § 2, 2°.

[4] De Clercq, *Traité de Droit Canonique,* II, n. 59.

[5] Woywod, *A Practical Commentary on the Code of Canon Law,* I, n. 673.

mental seat is not entitled to this privilege. Besides, the privilege may not be extended to those who have abdicated, or have been forced to cede the throne or governmental power.[6] Nor may it be retained by him who in a legitimate election has been supplanted by another as the principal head or ruler of a government. This privilege is conceded to those who are *de iure* first in government, although this title is more honorific than real. It is not enjoyed by dictators or prime ministers who *de facto* are acting rulers in a country, but who *de iure* hold a place of honor below the supreme head of a government.[7]

This concession as granted by the Code is restricted to the children or grandchildren of these actual or prospective rulers.[8] As a consequence, this privilege should not be extended to the children or grandchildren of those of noble lineage. Likewise, the Code clearly indicates that it is not a privilege to be enjoyed by wealthy people, or by powerful or influential persons in the government. Since, however, ecclesiastical law, in this regard, does not reprobate any existing custom contrary to the present legislation, any custom which existed prior to the Code, and which extended to nobles and other influential people the right of having their children and grandchildren baptized at home, can be tolerated by the ordinary, if circumstances require such an arrangement as a matter of prudent conduct.[9] In this matter, however, the bishop is the sole judge in each particular case concerning the conditions which will warrant the continuation of such a contrary custom.[10]

In particular, however, it is required that those who are entitled to this privilege should make a special petition for its use in each individual case. This petition for permission to have solemn baptism administered at home can be made either to the proper ordinary or to the proper pastor of those who desire to avail them-

---

[6] Claeys Bouuaert-Simenon, *Manuale Juris Canonici,* II, n. 53.

[7] Claeys Bouuaert-Simenon, *loc. cit.*

[8] Ayrinhac, *Legislation on the Sacraments,* n. 45.

[9] Canon 5.

[10] Coronata, *De Sacramentis,* I, n. 155; Noldin-Schmitt, *Summa Theologia Moralis,* III, n. 83; Lehmkuhl, *Theologia Moralis,* II, 52; Prümmer, *Manuale Theologiae Moralis,* III, 105.

selves of this privilege.[11] It is the prerogative of either the proper ordinary or the pastor licitly to administer solemn baptism at home under such circumstances,[12] or to delegate another priest to administer the sacrament. Thus this privilege does not inherently belong to the children and grandchildren of acting or prospective rulers, but it depends primarily on the petition made to the proper ordinary or pastor.[13] Consequently, solemn baptism may be licitly administered under such circumstances only when it is so requested from the proper authority.

On all occasions when the right of administering solemn baptism at home is employed, the sacrament should be conferred in a private oratory, if there is one in the house, or else in a suitable room of the residence. Since baptismal water should always be used in solemn baptism,[14] the pastor or delegated priest should bring along a small amount from the baptismal font of the parish church.[15]

SECT. II. IN PRIVATE HOUSES WITH THE PERMISSION OF THE ORDINARY

Another exception to the common norm that requires the administration of solemn baptism in a church or public oratory is conceded by the Code in so far as the ordinary for a just and reasonable cause and in an extraordinary case may permit the conferring of the sacrament in a private house.[16] For the concession of this permission it is necessary that there intervene the prudent deliberation of the ordinary, a just and reasonable cause, and an extraordinary case.[17]

The common norm should not yield to the whim of the pastor or to the desire of the parents who may seek to attain a distinction through the administration of solemn baptism in their home. Rather, it is the prerogative of only the ordinary to judge whether

---

[11] Blat, *Commentarium,* Lib. III, pars I, n. 66.

[12] Augustine, *A Commentary on the New Code of Canon Law,* IV, 92.

[13] Coronata, *De Sacramentis,* I, n. 155.

[14] Canon 757, § 1.

[15] Canon 776, § 2; Augustine, *op. cit.,* IV, 92.

[16] Canon 776, § 1, 2°.

[17] Blat, *Commentarium,* Lib. III, pars I, n. 66.

there are present such circumstances as warrant this exceptional permission. Before the promulgation of the Code the II Plenary Council of Baltimore (1866) left it to the prudent judgment of the missionaries to confer solemn baptism on children in their homes, when inclement weather, extreme hardship in travel or other grave causes were a serious obstacle to the solemn administration of the sacrament in a church.[18] In view of the more conservative norm laid down in the Code, it is evident that this particular law of the Council of Baltimore contravenes the universal law. Since this particular law is manifestly opposed to the law of the Code, and since the Code does not make any express provision for the continued application of this former particular law, it must be considered as abrogated.[19] As a consequence, even in cases of necessity other than danger of death the pastor is no longer authorized to decide whether there is sufficient reason for the conferring of solemn baptism at home. This judgment is now completely committed to the discretion of the ordinary.[20] Moreover, the Sacred Congregation of the Sacraments, in 1925, in a special reply, explicitly stated that the decision concerning the gravity of the extraordinary case is left to the prudence of the ordinary himself in each individual case.[21]

Although the decision for the administration of solemn baptism at home is left to the ordinary, yet it is not his prerogative to concede any general permission to the priests of his diocese, or, if he is a missionary bishop or a vicar apostolic, he cannot grant this same permission to the missionaries who labor in his territory. The granting of such a general permission is not in conformity with the intent of the Church's law, especially in view of the reply of the Sacred Congregation of the Sacraments, which explicitly stated that the ordinary could grant the permission only in individual

---

[18] *Acta et Decreta,* n. 237.

[19] Canon 6, 1°.

[20] Woywod, "Concerning the Faculty to Baptize in a Private House outside the Case of Danger of Death," *Homiletic and Pastoral Review,* XXVI (1925-26), 299.

[21] S. C. de Sacramentis *Romana et Aliarum,* 22 iul. 1925—*AAS,* XVII (1925), 452. Found in Bouscaren, *Canon Law Digest,* I, 347.

cases.[22] Ramstein maintains that if the local ordinary by general statute describes the conditions under which solemn baptism may be administered in private homes in his diocese, there is, then, no need to apply to the ordinary for permission in each case.[23] Such an opinion seems to be contrary to the enacted law, for the law in no way indicates that the ordinary has authorization for granting by statute a general permission to the priests of his diocese in such cases. In order that an ordinary may concede a general permission for solemn baptism in private houses, rather than have the priests of his diocese seek a special permission in each case, it is necessary that he apply to the Holy See for an indult. Without an indult for the granting of such a general permission he would be acting contrary to law. Such an indult could prove especially serviceable in missionary territory where the missionaries will frequently find great difficulty in seeking the special permission of the vicar apostolic in each individual case. In cases, not only in missionary territory but in our own country, which will allow no delay, and for which no general permission is lawfully granted in virtue of an indult, the pastor, or also another priest with the permission of the pastor, may presume the permission of the ordinary. In view of such circumstances, it seems that the priest would be compelled to use *epicheia,* and he would act lawfully by making use of this device which is in accord with the law.

In making his judgment, the ordinary must give special consideration to the cause involved. The law requires that it be a just and reasonable cause, but it does not demand that it be a very grave cause. In several circumstances a just and reasonable cause would exist. If a person, though he is not in danger of death, suffered from some infirmity which rendered it impossible for him to leave his home and go or be brought to a church, then he should obtain from the ordinary the permission to be baptized at home.[24] Again, because of the inclemency of the weather, a sickly child who is *de facto* not in danger of death at home might easily lapse into

---

[22] Woywod, "Baptism in Private Houses," *Homiletic and Pastoral Review,* XXV (1924-25), 647.

[23] *A Manual of Canon Law* (Hoboken, New Jersey: Terminal Printing and Publishing Co., 1948), p. 410.

[24] Ayrinhac, *Legislation on the Sacraments,* n. 45.

. such a danger if he is exposed to cold or damp air. In such a case he is entitled to receive the permission of the ordinary for solemn baptism at home.

Coronata[25] and Augustine[26] are of the opinion that if some prominent Catholic would request to have his children baptized in the house of a consul of his nation, as may occur among foreigners, then this would be an extraordinary case in which a just and reasonable cause would be present. Augustine believes that this permission would likewise be granted for the administration of solemn baptism in the palaces of Catholic ambassadors.[27] In the case of an illegitimate child, there certainly would be a just and reasonable cause for this permission in order to protect the family from a loss of reputation, were it to arise from the public fact of bringing such a child to a church for the administration of solemn baptism. In such a case the ceremony is not public, and the purpose of the priest's visit to the home need not be known.[28]

As long as the ordinary, in his prudent and conscientious deliberation, finds a just and reasonable cause in an extraordinary case, he may concede this permission. For a pastor or his delegate to administer solemn baptism in a private house without the permission of the ordinary and without a true just and reasonable cause would make its administration illicit.[29]

Under no circumstances may the administration of solemn baptism take place in the home of a non-Catholic.[30] In harmony with the mention made in the previous section, those who make use of this permission granted by the ordinary should make sure that either a private oratory, if there is one in the house, or at least a suitable room in the residence, is made available for the conferring of the solemn baptism. Moreover, the minister of the sacrament should confer it only with the regular baptismal water,[31] blessed on Holy Saturday or on the Vigil of Pentecost, or accord-

---

[25] *De Sacramentis,* I, n. 155.

[26] *A Commentary on the New Code of Canon Law,* IV, 92.

[27] *Op. cit.,* IV, p. 92, footnote 27.

[28] Lehmkuhl, *Theologia Moralis,* II, 52.

[29] Coronata, *De Sacramentis,* I, n. 155; Cappello, *De Sacramentis,* I, n. 187.

[30] S. C. S. Off. (Siam.), 21 ian. 1767, ad 1—*Collectanea Sacrae Congregationis de Propaganda Fide,* n. 465; *Fontes,* n. 819.

[31] Canon 776, § 2.

ing to the formula prescribed for the blessing of baptismal water when its supply has been exhausted. In addition to baptismal water, the priest should also bring along the holy oils required for the anointings which are prescribed for solemn baptism. In the absence of a private oratory, a table covered with a white cloth on which are placed two candles and an image of Our Lord should be set up in a suitable room, so that a sacred atmosphere will be present for the administration of the sacrament.[32]

SECT. III. IN OTHER PLACES NOT USUAL FOR THE ADMINISTRATION OF SOLEMN BAPTISM

From time to time there arises a situation which does not harmoniously lend itself to the atmosphere or the usual circumstances which the ecclesiastical legislator envisaged when he stated in the Code that the proper place for solemn baptism is a baptistery in a church or in a public oratory.[33] At times the baptistery or baptismal font in a church or public oratory may be unavailable, either because of the extensive renovation of the sacred edifice, or because of a fire or some other calamity. Perhaps, too, the use of the baptistery or the baptismal font would impose a grave hardship on either the minister of the sacrament or the person to be baptized. In particular, this would be the case in very cold weather when the church or the baptistery may not be heated. If the church is well heated, there should be no difficulty in conferring solemn baptism in it. Perhaps all that will be needed is to warm a small quantity of the baptismal water, in order to remove the chill that could cause considerable irritation when the water is applied to the sensitive skin of a child.

If, however, the church is so cold that it would be dangerous to the health of a child to baptize him there, then some other suitable place will have to be provided. The fact simply that the church is very cold will not suffice as a reason for warranting a postponement of baptism, which is to be administered *quamprimum*.[34] Since

[32] Barin, *Commentarium ad Canones Codicis Juris Canonici Jus Liturgicum Quocumque Modo Spectantes* (Rhodigii: Ex Officina Typographica Industrie Grafiche Italiane, 1922), p. 45.

[33] Canon 773.

[34] Canon 770.

a reasonable cause would exist for not conferring the sacrament in a church, the sacristy would be a very suitable place for the administration of solemn baptism in such a case.[35] Nevertheless, the approval of the ordinary should be obtained before the sacristy is employed for this purpose.[36]

If even the use of the sacristy would occasion danger for the health of a child, then some suitable room in the rectory could be used for the administration of the sacrament. In some places, because of the extreme cold and in order to avoid the great cost of heat by conserving fuel, the ordinaries permit the pastors to use some room in the rectory for a winter chapel during the week, when only a few people attend Mass. Under these conditions such a place could be used for the administration of solemn baptism. But before a room in the rectory is used for the conferring of the sacrament, the permission of the ordinary should be sought. For these peculiar circumstances the ordinary may provide by way of diocesan statute. Noldin (1838-1922)-Schmitt (1871-1948) claimed that there are diocesan rituals, approved by the Holy See, which permit baptism in the sacristy or in the rectory during severe cold weather.[37] In the absence of a statute providing for such a case, the pastor should judge whether a just and reasonable cause is present for administering solemn baptism in the sacristy or in the rectory, and in conjunction with the petition wherein he requests permission to baptize in one of these places he should inform the ordinary of this existing cause in order to obtain his approval.

A decree of the Sacred Congregation of Rites stated that the ordinary, in his prudent discretion, could permit the administration of solemn baptism before an altar instead of at the baptismal font. Such a permission could be occasioned when the parents on account of their special devotion to some saint, or also for the purpose of adding solemnity to the administration of the sacrament, ask to have their child baptized before an altar dedicated to that saint.[38]

---

[35] Prümmer, *Manuale Theologiae Moralis,* III, 105.

[36] S. R. C., *Sancti Iacobi de Cile,* 14 mart. 1861—*Fontes,* n. 6001; Ayrinhac, *Legislation on the Sacraments,* n. 45.

[37] *Summa Theologia Moralis,* III, n. 82.

[38] S. R. C., *Iacen.,* 1 sept. 1888—*Fontes,* n. 6191.

CHAPTER VIII

MISCELLANEOUS ITEMS

SECT. I. THE SUPPLYING OF THE CEREMONIES OF BAPTISM

There sometimes exists a case of necessity which demands that the essential matter and form necessary for the validity of baptism be administered without the ceremonies prescribed for the solemnity of the sacrament. Outside a case of necessity, however, it is never lawful to separate the ceremonies used in baptism from the application of the matter and form.[1] The general ecclesiastical law does not permit the omission of any of these baptismal ceremonies. It deviates from its general principle only in the case of adult converts from heresy who receive conditional baptism. In this case it concedes to the local ordinary the option of permitting the omission of these ceremonies.[2]

If private baptism has been conferred, then the omitted ceremonies should be supplied in church *quamprimum*.[3] Under ordinary circumstances the obligation of supplying these ceremonies is grave, and only a legitimate cause will excuse.[4] Moreover, there should be no unnecessary delay in the supplying of these ceremonies, but the recently baptized person should as soon as possible and at his earliest convenience have them supplied in church. This obligation exists not only for the time immediately following the reception of baptism, but it continues to exist even when there has been a necessary delay or notable procrastination extending over a long period of time. In the case of adults the ordinary can dispense for a grave cause and in certain cases.[5]

Since the proper place for the administration of solemn bap-

---

[1] St. Alphonsus, *Theologia Moralis,* Lib. VI, n. 141 (2 vols., Taurini: Marietti, 1878), II, p. 208.

[2] Canon 759, § 2.

[3] Canon 759, § 3.

[4] Cappello, *De Sacramentis,* I, n. 175.

[5] Coronata, *De Sacramentis,* I, n. 141.

tism is a church or a public oratory,[6] it must *a pari* be reasoned that the proper place for the supplying of the baptismal ceremonies is a church or a public oratory.[7] Furthermore, since the lawful minister of the sacrament is the proper pastor of the person to be baptized, and since the parochial church of the parish to which the recipient of baptism is attached is the proper place for the administration of solemn baptism, it must be inferred that the parochial church is also the proper place for the administering of these supplementary ceremonies. Thus when a child or an adult receives private baptism outside the territory of his proper parish, it is manifest that the pastor of the parish within which the hospital is located does not also acquire a right to supply the ceremonies of baptism. In the case of private baptism, urgency may demand that a priest other than the proper pastor baptize the dying child or adult in the hospital or at home, but after the private baptism is conferred there is no longer any similar urgency for the supplying of the ceremonies of solemn baptism.

Nevertheless, there may exist an exceptional case in which the local pastor would be justified in supplying the ceremonies which under normal circumstances are to be supplied by the proper pastor in the parochial church of the baptized person. Such would be the case when the child is so far recuperated that he could be brought to the local parish church, but not to his proper parish church, and there still persists for the child a danger of death until the time that he can be brought to his proper parish church. It may be argued that these ceremonies are not necessary for salvation, and, moreover, that there can readily exist a just cause for deferring them longer than for postponing the baptism itself. Nevertheless, the Church desires that these ceremonies be supplied after baptism, so that in a case in which there is constituted a danger of death the rights of the proper pastor should yield to the spiritual good which the child will derive from these ceremonies.

When it is necessary to omit any of the ceremonies preceding baptism, then all of them should be omitted, even the anointing

---

[6] Canon 773.

[7] Augustine, *A Commentary on the New Code of Canon Law,* IV, 72.

with the Holy Oils, since all these ceremonies must be performed according to the form prescribed in the *Ritual*.[8] If, however, a priest or a deacon is the minister of private baptism, then he should observe the ceremonies consequent to the act of baptism, provided that the person baptized still continues alive.[9] When the danger of death has ceased, the remaining ceremonies should later be supplied in the parish church.[10] The Sacred Congregation of Rites directed that in the conferring of private baptism in a hospital or in a private house the priest should not wear a purple stole or anoint a dying infant with the Oil of Catechumens. Rather, in a case of necessity all ceremonies should be omitted which precede the act of baptizing.[11]

When it is convenient to the priest, he should bring along baptismal water for the administration of private baptism. If the priest does not have the time to obtain some baptismal water and bring it along with him to the hospital or to the private house because of an extreme danger of death, then he can baptize with ordinary water as a lay person would do in such a case.[12] Although chrism is required for the anointing prescribed in the ceremonies consequent to baptism, the priest may not always have time to obtain it when an extreme emergency demands his immediate presence for the administration of private baptism, and thus he has no obligation to anoint with chrism in such a case. Because one case differs from another, the priest should conscientiously judge in each case whether there is time to bring along the chrism. The question of whether the priest can employ the ceremonies of the white cloth and candle without the anointing with chrism has not yet received an authentic interpretation. It is believed that the priest can use these ceremonies without chrism, if he wishes, but he has no obligation to do so.[13]

---

[8] *Rituale Romanum*, tit. II, c. 5.

[9] Canon 759, § 1.

[10] Noldin-Schmitt, *Summa Theologiae Moralis*, III, n. 83.

[11] S. R. C., *Calceaten.*, 23 sept. 1820—*Decreta Authentica Congregationis Sacrorum Rituum*, n. 2607.

[12] Barin, *Commentarium ad Canones Codicis Juris Canonici Jus Liturgicum Quocumque Modo Spectantes*, p. 31.

[13] Barin, *op. cit.*, p. 32.

When perchance all the ceremonies were performed at an infant's presentation for baptism, but the act of baptizing itself remained invalid, then only the essential rite need later to be conferred.[14] But in the case of an infant baptized by a heretical minister, the ceremonies prescribed for the solemn baptism of infants should always be supplied, whether or not the infant receives a conditional baptism.[15]

If for an adult who received private baptism in the Catholic Church during infancy the ceremonies have not yet been supplied, then the formula of the ceremonies is that which is prescribed for the baptism of infants.[16] When an adult, however, is a convert from a heretical sect and a conditional baptism remains to be conferred, then the ceremonies need not be supplied if the ordinary has conceded permission for the administration of conditional baptism without the ceremonies.[17] On the other hand, if for an adult convert the ceremonies are also supplied along with the conferring of the conditional baptism, or if the ceremonies are supplied apart from any conditional baptism, then the ceremonies are those which are to be observed in the baptism of adults,[18] but the local ordinary, for a grave and reasonable cause, can permit that the ceremonies prescribed for the baptism of infants be employed in the baptism of adults.[19] Again, if the convert was never validly baptized, then baptism must be administered absolutely, and the ceremonies prescribed in the baptism of adults must be observed, unless the local ordinary for a grave cause has conceded permission to use the formula of infant baptism.[20] When, however, through an error there has occurred a notable omission of some rite or ceremonies, such as the anointing with the Holy Oils, then this omission must be supplied, unless great difficulty stands in the way of the effort to do so. If

---

[14] Noldin-Schmitt, *loc. cit.*

[15] Lehmkuhl, *Theologia Moralis,* II, 53.

[16] Coronata, *De Sacramentis,* I, n. 141; S. R. C., *Rhedonen.,* 27 aug. 1836, ad 3—*Decreta Authentica Congregationis Sacrorum Rituum,* n. 2743.

[17] Canon 759, § 2.

[18] Lehmkuhl, *loc. cit.*

[19] Canon 755, § 2; Noldin, *Summa Theologiae Moralis,* III, n. 83.

[20] Woywod, *A Practical Commentary on the Code of Canon Law,* II, n. 653

the error is discovered before the godparents depart with the infant, it can easily be corrected. If it is adverted to only after the departure of the baptized child or adult, then the difficulty attendant upon a return for the correcting of this error, or the scandal which perhaps might arise, will excuse the minister of the sacrament from the obligation of making the correction.[21]

SECT. II. THE REGISTRATION OF BAPTISM

Since baptism constitutes the necessary foundation for the reception of the other sacraments, it is particularly necessary that special stress be placed upon the importance of positively and properly registering the facts, such as the time and the place, which are pertinent to the reception of baptism. The Code decrees that every pastor must maintain a baptismal register,[22] in regard to which he has the grave obligation to exercise special supervision.[23]

Since the licit administration of baptism is reserved to the proper pastor of the subject,[24] and since the parochial church of the parish in which the adult has a domicile or quasi-domicile, or, in the case of an infant, the parish in which his father has a domicile, is the proper place of baptism,[25] it follows that the record of baptism will generally be kept in the proper parish of the person baptized. But in consequence of various circumstances it frequently occurs that the minister of the sacrament is not the proper pastor, and that the proper parochial church of the baptized person is not the place of baptism. When a child cannot easily and without delay be brought to his proper pastor and parish church for solemn baptism, the Code permits another pastor in his own territory to administer the sacrament.[26] Now, the record of baptism must be kept in the parish where the person was baptized,[27] and thus the obligation of making the registration

---

[21] Noldin-Schmitt, *Summa Theologiae Moralis,* III, n. 82.

[22] Canon 470, § 1.

[23] Cappello, *De Sacramentis,* I, n. 183.

[24] Canons 462, 1° and 738, § 1.

[25] Canon 774, § 1.

[26] Canon 738, § 2.

[27] Canon 777, § 1.

devolves upon the pastor of the parish where the baptism was licitly administered. If a priest other than the pastor was the minister of baptism, his name must be inscribed, and not that of the pastor of the church.[28] Moreover, in the case of private baptism, if a priest distinct from the minister of the sacrament assists at the supplying of the ceremonies, his name is also to be recorded.[29]

The pastor who has baptized a person not belonging to his parish is obliged to inform the proper pastor as soon as possible.[30] This he can do either personally or by mail. If the baptized person should, perchance, have several proper pastors, the minister of baptism need not inform everyone of them, but simply the one in whose parish the baptized has actual domicile at the time of the reception of the sacrament, or in whose parish the father has actual domicile at the time of the baptism of the infant. In a private response, the Sacred Congregation of the Council stated that the parish priest who administers baptism should register the facts and should send the proper pastor a simple notification.[31] Neither canon 778 nor the *Roman Ritual* prescribes in detail what form this notification should take. Strictly taken, a simple notice with the necessary data would satisfy, but a mere private letter would not be sufficient. The notification should have the form of an official document with pastoral signature and parochial seal.[32] When this notification must be sent to a pastor of a diocese other than that in which the sacrament was administered, it should be sent through the chancery of the diocese *a qua*, i.e., the chancery of the diocese in which the sacrament was conferred.[33] *Vagi,* who have neither a domicile nor a quasi-domicile, are to be baptized

[28] O'Rourke, *Parish Registers,* The Catholic University of America Canon Law Studies, n. 88 (Washington, D. C.: The Catholic University of America, 1934), p. 48.

[29] O'Rourke, *loc. cit.*

[30] Canon 778.

[31] S. C. C., 31 ian. 1927—Bouscaren, *Canon Law Digest,* II, 184.

[32] O'Rourke, *Parish Registers,* p. 49.

[33] Augustine, *A Commentary on the New Code of Canon Law,* V, 312; cf. Instruction, S. C. Sacr., 29 iun., 1941, ad 4 a—Bouscaren, *Canon Law Digest,* II, 255.

in the parish where they actually reside, and the fact of their baptism is to be registered in only that parish.[34]

After the proper pastor has obtained the notification of the administration of baptism to one of his subjects, he has the obligation to enter the record of such a baptism in the baptismal register of his parish which is the parish of origin for the baptized person.[35]

Just how long a time is allowed for a transmitting of the notification of baptism to the proper pastor depends upon the interpretation of *quamprimum* in canon 778. Augustine did not determine any definite time for the sending of the notice, as long as there was eliminated any voluntary procrastination,[36] while Blat considers a few days' delay, under ordinary circumstances, to involve but a slight violation of the law.[37] O'Rourke[38] believes that the term *quamprimum* permits only three or four days as the widest extension of time for the transmitting of this notification.[39]

In regard to the administration of private baptism in a hospital which does not have a resident chaplain. the registration of baptism should be made in the baptismal record of the parish within the territory of which the hospital is located. The information for the register is to be supplied by the local parish priest, who generally also is the one who conferred the sacrament, or by the lay person who conferred it when extreme necessity did not permit any delay until the arrival of the priest. If the hospital has a resident chaplain, then it seems quite feasible for the hospital to possess its own baptismal register, in which the chaplain could then enter the records of any baptism administered in the institution. Having done this, the chaplain should send an authentic copy of the entry to the local parish and also to the proper pastor of the baptized person. Such a procedure may be indicated through di-

---

[34] Woywod, "Recording of Baptism Conferred outside Proper Parish," *Homiletic and Pastoral Review,* XLI (1940-1941), 87.

[35] Cf. Instruction S. C. Sacr., 29 iun. 1941, ad 11 d—Bouscaren, *op. cit.,* II, 263.

[36] *A Commentary on the New Code of Canon Law,* V, 312.

[37] *Commentarium,* lib. III, pars I, n. 69.

[38] *Parish Registers,* p. 49.

[39] Cf. Waldron, *The Minister of Baptism,* p. 175.

ocesan legislation, as is the case in the statutes of at least one archdiocese in the United States.[40] If, perchance, a baptismal font has been erected in a hospital chapel, there certainly should be a baptismal register in that institution for the recording of the administration of solemn baptism. In such a case the chaplain, after he has registered the baptism, should notify the proper pastor in whose parish the parent of the infant or the adult patient has a domicile. Provision can be made for this by means of particular legislation, as already is the case in one diocese.[41]

When a church has acquired a cumulative right with other churches of administering solemn baptism to all those who live within a certain parochial district,[42] then it should *a pari* have its own baptismal register for the recording of all such administrations of the sacrament. In addition to making the registration, the pastor or rector of the church must notify the proper pastor of the recipient.[43] When the ordinary either permits or directs that a baptismal font be placed in a non-parochial church or in a public oratory for the accommodation of the people,[44] then it seems proper that the pastor of the parish, who still retains the right to baptize all who are brought to such a church or oratory, should record these baptisms in the parish register. Under such circumstances a non-parochial church or public oratory would not have to keep any special registry of its own. Again, if the ordinary, on account of a grave inconvenience or danger, permits solemn baptism to be conferred by the local pastor in a non-parochial church or public oratory which has no baptismal font,[45] the registration of the baptism should be made in the baptismal register of the local parish. This rule will apply *a fortiori* to the case in which the ordinary permits the administration of solemn baptism in a house for a just and reasonable cause in some extra-

---

[40] *Synodal Statutes of the Archdiocese of Newark* (Arlington, N. J.: Catholic Protectory Press, 1941), n. 87.

[41] *Synodus Dioecesana Fargensis Prima* (Milwauchiae: Bruce, 1941), n. 222.

[42] Canon 774, § 1.

[43] Canon 778.

[44] Canon 774, § 2.

[45] Canon 775.

ordinary circumstances.[46] The priest who administers the sacrament must see to the recording of the fact of the baptism in the registry of the church within the territory of which the house is located.

SECT. III. STOLE FEES

In determining that the administration of solemn baptism is reserved to the pastor,[47] and that the baptismal font in the parochial church of the recipient is the proper place for the conferring of the sacrament, the Code does not reflect any particular enactment regarding the offering made on the occasion of a baptism. As a consequence, in the absence of any general ecclesiastical legislation, the legitimate norms concerning such an offering must be determined by particular statute or custom.[48]

The II Plenary Council of Baltimore (1866) prohibited priests from requesting money for the administration of the sacraments, but it explicitly permitted the acceptance of voluntary offerings at the time of baptism.[49] In connection with this fact, it directed that the ordinary should establish a just method for the distributing of such offerings among the clergy of the same rectory. Special consideration was to be given to the pastor.[50] Thus the Council recommended that the pastor should share the baptismal stole fees with his assistants. Since the promulgation of the Code all determinations regarding stole fees are to be made by a provincial council,[51] and the law does not permit to pastors any departure from the established norms. If a pastor does exceed these norms, he is bound to restitution.[52] In the event, however, that a person is unable or unwilling to make an offering, the minister of the sacrament is rightfully expected to furnish a gratuitous administration.[53]

---

[46] Canon 776, § 1, 2°.
[47] Canon 462, 1°.
[48] Waldron, *The Minister of Baptism,* p. 177.
[49] *Acta et Decreta,* n. 221.
[50] *Ibid.,* n. 94.
[51] Canon 1507.
[52] Canon 463, § 2.
[53] Canon 463, § 4.

In regard to the assignment of the baptismal offering, the proper pastor of the recipient of baptism has a right to the offering made on the occasion of the administration of the sacrament, and the pastor who baptizes the subject of another pastor without the latter's expressed or presumed permission, except in the face of a positive necessity, is obliged to restore the stole fee to the proper pastor whose right he usurped.[54] Even in the administration of baptism if a priest acts for the pastor and in his parish church with either his expressed or presumed permission, nevertheless the offering made on the occasion of the baptism belongs to the pastor.[55] When, however, in a manifest case of necessity, a priest baptizes the subject of another pastor, inasmuch as the recipient cannot be brought to his proper parish church without inconvenience and delay,[56] then the ministering priest is entitled to the offering made on the occasion of the baptism. In this case of necessity the pastor of the parish where the person is actually sojourning receives authorization from the Church's law to confer baptism, and to receive and retain the offering.[57]

When a person is baptized in a church which has an acquired cumulative right to baptize persons from parishes comprised within a certain district over which the right of this church extends,[58] then the pastor or rector of this church has the right to retain the stole fees given to him at the time of the administration of baptism.[59] Moreover, when custom or statute permits a priest to baptize all the converts whom he has instructed, he shares the full right of receiving the offering.[60]

If a hospital, when withdrawn from the jurisdiction of the local pastor,[61] has a chaplain who is entitled to function *pleno*

---

[54] Plenary Council of Baltimore (1866), *Acta et Decreta,* n. 227.

[55] Canon 463, § 3; Woywod, *A Practical Commentary on the Code of Canon Law,* I, n. 633.

[56] Canon 738, § 2.

[57] Ferry, *Stole Fees,* The Catholic University of America Canon Law Studies, n. 59 (Washington, D. C.: The Catholic University of America, 1930), p. 66.

[58] Canon 774, § 1.

[59] Ferry, *op. cit.,* p. 67.

[60] Waldron, *The Minister of Baptism,* p. 179.

[61] Canon 464, § 2.

iure, and if a baptismal font has been erected in the chapel of the institution, then the chaplain who administers solemn baptism is entitled also to retain the baptismal offering. This, however, is not the case when solemn baptism is administered in some other non-parochial church or public oratory furnished with a baptismal font,[62] and *a fortiori* when the sacrament is conferred in such places if not furnished with a font. Though in these instances the permission of the ordinary was given for the accommodation of the faithful,[63] the pastor of the parish within the territory of which the church or the oratory is situated remains the lawful minister of baptism in these places, and consequently he is entitled to the baptismal offering. Likewise, the pastor is entitled to the offering given on the occasion of the administration of solemn baptism in a private house with the permission of the ordinary for a just and reasonable cause and in an extraordinary case.[64]

[62] Canon 774, § 2.

[63] Canon 775.

[64] Canon 776, § 1, 2°.

CONCLUSIONS

(1) During the time of a general local interdict solemn baptism may be administered in the cathedral and in parish churches, unless it is expressly stated otherwise in the decree of the interdict.

(2) In regard to the proper days for the administration of solemn baptism, the Code imposes no obligation, but it merely makes a recommendation. As a consequence, any reasonable cause will justify the conferring of solemn baptism on any other day than the vigils of Easter and Pentecost.

(3) Since there may exist many reasons which would make it very inconvenient or would even prevent an adult from immediately attending Mass and receiving Holy Communion, he may receive the sacrament in the afternoon or evening and fulfill these two precepts on the following morning or even within several days of the reception of baptism.

(4) A grave obligation exists for parents to have their children baptized at least within a month after birth, and only for a reasonable cause and under extraordinary circumstances may they defer baptism from one to two months.

(5) It is within the power of the ordinary to determine by diocesan statute the exact number of days within which the grave obligation of baptizing infants must be fulfilled.

(6) Pastors should not refuse or defer the baptism of children of lapsed Catholic parents when they are brought by these parents or by Catholic sponsors with the parents' consent, provided there is expressed a willingness, which is accompanied with some possible hope, that the children will be reared and educated in the Catholic faith.

(7) Valid baptism cannot be administered in the womb, unless the membranes of the fetus are ruptured and the amniotic fluid discharged, and, moreover, baptism cannot be conferred validly upon the umbilical cord.

(8) The Code permits to a public oratory the lawful possession

of a font, but it neither explicitly nor implicitly extends this permission to semipublic oratories.

(9) Concession of permission for the administration of solemn baptism in a non-parochial church or public oratory without a font is not the exclusive prerogative of the ordinary, for the pastor is not in any way required either to seek the ordinary's permission or to notify him of the exercise of the right.

(10) Inasmuch as a hospital chapel is generally a semipublic oratory, the ordinary should apply to the Holy See for an indult conceding the erection of a baptismal font in such an oratory, when occasions requiring the administration of solemn baptism occur frequently. If the occasions requiring the administration of solemn baptism are infrequent, the permission of the ordinary should be sought in each case in order that the sacrament may be licitly conferred in a semipublic oratory which does not possess a font.

(11) It is not the prerogative of the ordinary to concede by diocesan statute or in any other way a general permission to the priest of his diocese for the conferring of solemn baptism in a private house.

(12) Provided there is a just and reasonable cause, the pastor, in the absence of a diocesan statute, should obtain the permission of the ordinary for the administration of solemn baptism in the sacristy or in the rectory.

(13) The parochial church is the proper place for the supplying of the ceremonies of baptism.

(14) If a baptismal font has been erected in a hospital chapel, it should possess its own baptismal register, and the chaplain of the hospital should send notification of the baptism to the proper pastor of the baptized subject. The proper pastor, then, has the obligation to enter the record of such a baptism in the baptismal register of his parish church.

(15) If a chaplain who has the right to function *pleno iure* administers solemn baptism in the chapel of a hospital in which a font has been erected, he is entitled to retain the baptismal offering.

BIBLIOGRAPHY

Sources

Acta Apostolicae Sedis, Commentarium Officiale, Romae, 1909—.

Acta et Decreta Concilii Plenarii Americae Latinae in Urbe Celebrati Anno Domini MDCCCXCIX, Romae, 1902.

Acta et Decreta Sacrorum Conciliorum Recentiorum, Collectio Lacensis, 7 vols., Friburgi Brisgoviae, 1870-1892.

Acta Sanctae Sedis, 41 vols., Romae, 1865-1908.

Bouscaren, T. Lincoln, *Canon Law Digest,* 2 vols. and *Supplement through 1948,* Milwaukee: The Bruce Publishing Company, 1934-1949.

Bruns, Herm. Theod., *Canones Apostolorum et Conciliorum Saeculorum IV-VII,* 2 vols., Berolini, 1839.

Catholic Encyclopedia, The, 15 vols., with Index and 2 Supplements, New York, 1907-1922.

Codicis Iuris Canonici Fontes cura Emi Petri Card. Gasparri editi, 9 vols., Romae later Civitate Vaticanae: Typis Polyglottis Vaticanis, 1923-1939 (Vols. VII, VIII et IX, ed. cura et studio Emi Iustiniani Card. Serédi).

Collectanea S. Congregationis de Propaganda Fide, 2 vols., Romae, Typographia Polyglotta S. C. de Propaganda Fide, 1907.

Concilii Plenarii Baltimorensis II, in Ecclesia Metropolitana Baltimorensi, a die VII, ad diem XXI Octobris, A. D. MDCCCLXVI Habiti et a Sede Apostolica Recogniti Acta et Decreta, Baltimorae: John Murphy, 1868.

Corpus Iuris Canonici, editio Lipsiensis secunda, post Aemilii Richteri curas . . . instruxit Aemilius Friedberg, 2 vols., Lipsiae: ex Officina Bernhardi Tauchnitz, 1879-1881. Editio anastatice repetita, Lipsiae: Tauchnitz, 1928.

Corpus Scriptorum Ecclesiasticorum Latinorum, Vindobonae, 1866—.

Decreta Authentica Congregationis Sacrorum Rituum ex Actis eiusdem Collecta eiusque Auctoritate promulgata sub Auspiciis Ss. Domini nostri Leonis Papae XIII, 5 vols. et 2 Appendices, Romae: ex Typographia Polyglotta, 1898-1927.

De Synodo Dioecesana, Libri XIII, 2 vols., Parmae: ex Typographia Fratrum Borsi, 1764.

Enchiridion Symbolorum et Definitionum de Rebus Fide et Morum. Denzinger-C. Bannwart-J. B. Umberg, editio 21-23, Friburgi Brisgoviae: Herder and Co., 1937.

Hardouin, Jean, *Acta Conciliorum et Epistolae Decretales ac Constitutiones Summorum Pontificum,* 12 vols., Parisiis, 1715.

Jaffé, Philippus, *Regesta Pontificum Romanorum ab condita Ecclesia ad annum post Christum natum MCXCVIII,* 2. ed. correctam et auctam auspiciis Gulielmi Wattenbach curaverunt S. Loewenfeld, F. Kaltenbrunner, P. Ewald, 2 vols. in 1, Lipsiae, 1885-1888.

Labbeus, Philippus, et Cossartius, Gabriel, *Sacrosancta Concilia ad Regiam Editionem Exacta,* 15 vols. in 16, Parisiis, 1671-1674.

Mansi, J. P., *Sacrorum Conciliorum Nova et Amplissima Collectio,* 53 vols. in 59, Parisiis-Arnhemii-Lipsiae, 1901-1927.

Monumenta Germaniae Historica, Hannoverae, 1826—

———, *Leges in 4,* Sectio II (*Capitularia Regum Francorum*), Tom. I, ed. A. Boretius, 1883.

———, *Epistolae* (*Ep.*), 7 vols., 1887-1928, Tom. III, ed. E. Dümmler, 1899; Tom. VI, ed. E. Perels, 1925.

Rituale Romanum Pauli V Pontificis Maximi iussu editum aliorumque Pontificum cura recognitum atque auctoritate SS̃mi D. N. Pii Papae Xi ad normam Codicis Iuris Canonici Accomodatum, Editio iuxta Typicam Vaticanam, Mechliniae: Typis H. Dessain, 1926.

Schroeder, H. J., *Canons and Decrees of the Council of Trent: Original Text with English Translation,* St. Louis: B. Herder Book Co., 1941.

Synodus Diocesana Fargensis Prima, Milwauchiae, Bruce, 1941.

Synodal Statutes of the Archdiocese of Newark, Arlington, N. J.: Catholic Protectory Press. 1941.

Thesaurus Resolutionum S. C. Concilii ab anno 1718, 167 vols., Urbini, 1718-1741; Romae, 1741-1908.

Reference Works

Aertnys, Joseph, *Compendium Liturgiae Sacrae,* 11. ed., Romae: Domus Editorialis Marietti, Sanctae Sedis Apostolicae et Sacrae Rituum Congregationis Typographi, 1943.

Aertnys, Joseph-Damen, C. A., *Theologia Moralis,* 13. ed., 2 vols., Taurini: Marietti, 1939.

Alphonsus, St., *Theologia Moralis,* 2 vols., Taurini: Marietti, 1878.

Aquinas, St. Thomas, *Summa Theologica,* ed. Marietti, 6 vols., Taurini, Romae: Marietti, 1937.

Attwater, Donald, *A Catholic Dictionary,* 12th printing, New York: The Macmillan Company, 1945.

Augustine, Charles, *A Commentary on the New Code of Canon Law,* 8 vols., St. Louis: B. Herder Book Co., 1931.

Ayrinhac, H. A., *Legislation on the Sacraments in the New Code of Canon Law,* New York: Longmans, Green and Co., 1928.

Barbosa, Augustine, *Collectanea Decretorum tam Veterum quam Recentiorum, in Ius Pontificium Universum,* 6 vols. in 3, Lugduni, 1715.

Barin, Aloisius, *Commentarium ad Canones Codicis Juris Canonici Jus Liturgicum Quocumque Modo Spectantes,* Rhodigii: Ex Officina Typographia Industrie Grafiche Italiane, 1922.

Beste, Udalricus, *Introductio in Codicem,* 3. ed., Collegeville, Minn.: St. John's Abbey Press, 1946.

Bingham, Joseph, *The Antiquities of the Christian Church,* edited by the Reverend Robert Bingham, 10 vols., Oxford, 1885.

———, *Dictionnaire d'archeologie chretienne et de liturgie,* 14 vols., incomplete, Paris, 1907—.

Blat, Albertus, *Commentarium Textus Codicis Iuris Canonici,* 5 vols. in 6, Romae: ex Typographia Pontificia in Instituto Pii IX, 1919-1927.

Bonnar, A., *The Catholic Doctor,* 2. ed., New York: P. J. Kenedy and Sons, 1939.

Bouuaert, F. C.-Simenon, G., *Manuale Juris Canonici,* 3 vols., Vol. II, 3. ed., Gandae et Leodii: Dessain, 1931.

Bowen, John, *Baptism of the Infant and Fetus, an Outline for the Use of Doctors and Nurses,* 4. ed., Dubuque: The M. J. Knippel Co., 1939.

Capellmann, Carl, *Medicina Pastoralis,* 7. ed., Aquisgrani: Rudolphus Barth, 1890.

Caponi, Julius, *Institutiones Canonicae,* 2. ed., 2 vols. in 1, Coloniae Allobrogum, 1734.

Cappello, F. M., *Tractatus Canonico-Moralis de Sacramentis,* 5 vols., Vol. I, 5. ed., Romae: Marietti, 1947.

Connolly, Nicholas P., *The Canonical Erection of Parishes,* The Catholic University of America Canon Law Studies, n. 114, Washington, D. C.: The Catholic University of America, 1938.

Conran, Edward, *The Interdict,* The Catholic University of America Canon Law Studies, n. 56, Washington, D. C.: The Catholic University of America, 1930.

Corblet, Jules, *Histoire dogmatique, liturgique, et archéologique du sacrement de baptême,* 2 vols., Paris, 1881-1882.

Coronata, Matthaeus Conte a, *Institutiones Iuris Canonici, De Sacramentis Tractatus Canonicus,* 3 vols., Taurini: Marietti, 1943-1946.

Costello, John, *Domicile and Quasi-Domicile,* The Catholic University of America Canon Law Studies, n. 60, Washington, D. C.: The Catholic University of America, 1930.

Davis, Henry, *Moral and Pastoral Theology,* 4. ed., 4 vols., New York: Sheed and Ward, 1945.

De Clercq, Charles, *Traité de Droit Canonique,* Publie sous la direction de Raoul Naz, 4 vols., Paris: Letouzey et Ané, 1948.

Dictionnaire de droit canonique, 4 vols. and 2 fascicles, incomplete, Paris: Letouzey et Ané, 1924—.

Dictionnaire de théologie catholique, 15 vols., incomplete, Paris: Letouzey et Ané, 1903—.

Drumm, William, *Hospital Chaplains,* The Catholic University of America Canon Law Studies, n. 178, Washington, D. C.: The Catholic University of America Press, 1943.

Fagnanus, Prosper, *Commentaria in Quinque Libros Decretalium,* 3 vols., Venetiis, 1709.

Fanfani, L., *De Iure Parochorum,* Romae: Marietti, 1924.

Feldhaus, A. H., *Oratories,* The Catholic University of America Canon Law Studies, n. 42, Washington, D. C.: The Catholic University of America, 1927.

Ferry, William, *Stole Fees,* The Catholic University of America Canon Law Studies, n. 59, Washington, D. C.: The Catholic University of America, 1930.

Funk, F. X., *Didascalia et Constitutiones Apostolorum,* 2 vols., Paderbornae, 1905.

Genicot, E., *Institutiones Theologiae Moralis,* 2 vols., Lovanii: Typis et Sumptibus Polleunis et Ceuterick, 1897.

Giraldi, Ubaldus, *Expositio Iuris Pontificii iuxta Recentiorem Ecclesiae Disciplinam,* nova romana editio, 2 vols., Romae, 1829-1830.

Glimm, F., Marique, J., and Walsh, G., *The Apostolic Fathers,* New York: Cima Publishing Co., 1947.

Goettelmann, Paul, *The Baptistery of Frejus,* Washington, D. C.: The Catholic University of America, 1933.

Goodwine, Joseph, *The Reception of Converts,* The Catholic University of America Canon Law Studies, n. 198, Washington, D. C.: The Catholic University of America Press, 1944.

Imbart de la Tour, Pierre, *De Ecclesiis Rusticanis Aetate Carolingica,* Parisiis, 1890.

Kenrick, Francis, *Treatise on Baptism,* Baltimore, 1852.

Koudelka, Charles, *Pastors, Their Rights and Duties According to the New Code of Canon Law,* The Catholic University of America Canon Law Studies, n. 11, Washington, D. C.: The Catholic University of America, 1921.

Kurtscheid, Bertrandus, *Historia Iuris Canonici, Historia Institutorum,* Romae: Vol. I (*ab Ecclesiae Fundationeusque ad Gratianum*), Romae: Officium Libri Catholici, 1941.

Lancelotti, Joannes, *Institutiones Iuris Canonici,* Venetiis, 1704.

Lehmkuhl, A., *Theologia Moralis,* 9. ed., 2 vols., Friburgi Brisgoviae, 1898.

Martène, Edmundus, *De Antiquis Ecclesiae Ritibus,* 4 vols., Rotomagi, 1700.

Martigny, Jean A., *Dictionnaire des Antiquites Chrétiennes,* Paris, 1855.

McAllister, Joseph, *Emergency Baptism,* Milwaukee: Bruce Publishing Company, 1945.

McFadden, Charles, *Medical Ethics,* 2. ed., Philadelphia: F. A. Davis Company, 1949.

Merkelbach, B. H., *Summa Theologiae Moralis,* ed. alt., 3 vols., Parisiis: Desclée, de Brouwer et Cie, 1939.

Migne, J. P., *Patrologiae Cursus Completus, Series Graeca,* 161 vols., Paris, 1857-1866.

———, *Patrologiae Cursus Completus, Series Latina,* 221 vols., Paris, 1844-1864.

Mothon, Jos. Pie, *Institutions Canoniques,* 3 vols., Paris: Desclee, de Brouwer et Cie, 1922-1924.

Moretti, Aloisius, *De Sacris Functionibus, Episcopo, Celebrante, Assistente, Absente,* 4 vols., Taurini: Marietti, 1936-1939.

Noldin, *Summa Theologiae Moralis,* 5. ed., Oeniponte: Typis et Sumptibus Fe., Rausch, F. Pustet, 1904-1905.

Noldin H.-Schmitt, A., *Summa Theologiae Moralis,* 26. ed., 3 vols., Ratisbonae: Fridericus Pustet, 1940.

O'Kane, James-Fallon, Michael, *Notes on the Rubrics of the Roman Ritual,* new edition completely revised in accordance with the latest 1925 *Editio Typica* of the *Rituale Romanum* and the Decrees of the Sacred Congregationis, Dublin: James Duffy and Co., Ltd., 1938.

O'Rourke, James, *Parish Registers,* The Catholic University of America Canon Law Studies, n. 88, Washington, D. C.: The Catholic University of America, 1934.

Pignatelli, Jacobus, *Consultationes Canonicae,* 6 vols., Coloniae Allobrogum, 1700.

Prümmer, D. M., *Manuale Theologiae Moralis,* 2. et 3. ed., 3 vols., Friburgi Brisgoviae, 1923.

Ramstein, Matthew, *A Manual of Canon Law,* Hoboken, New Jersey: Terminal Printing and Publishing Co., 1948.

Reichel, Oswald, *A Complete Manual of Canon Law,* Vol. I, *The Sacraments,* London, 1896.

Risi, Franciscus, *De Baptismo Parvulorum in Primitiva Ecclesia,* Romae, 1870.

Sabatier, Paul, *La Didache,* Paris, 1885.

Sabetti, A.-Barrett, T., *Compendium Theologiae Moralis,* 27. ed., New York: Frederick Pustet Co., Inc., 1919.

Schmalzgrueber, Franciscus, *Ius Ecclesiasticum Universum,* 5 vols. in 12, Romae, 1843-1845.

Sipos, Stephanus, *Enchiridion Iuris Canonici,* 3. ed., Pécs: ex Typographia "Haladas R. T.," 1936.

Smith, W., and Cheetham, S., *Dictionary of Christian Antiquities,* 2 vols., Toronto, 1880.

Suarez, F., *Opera Omnia,* 26 vols. in 28, editio nova a Carola Berton, Paris, apud Ludovicum Vives, 1856-1868.

Thomassinus, Ludovicus, *Vetus et Nova Ecclesiae Disciplina,* 3 vols., Parisiis, 1688.

Vermeersch, A.-Creusen, J., *Epitome Iuris Canonici,* 3 vols., vol. I, 6. ed., 1937; vol. II, 5. ed., 1934; vol. III, 5. ed., 1936, Mechliniae-Romae: H. Dessain.

Vermeersch, A., *Theologiae Moralis Principia, Responsa, Consilia,* 4 vols., 3. ed., Roma: Universitá Gregoriana, 1933-1937.

Waldron, Joseph, *The Minister of Baptism,* The Catholic University of America Canon Law Studies, n. 170, Washington, D. C.: The Catholic University of America Press, 1942.

Wernz, F.-Vidal, P., *Ius Canonicum,* 7 vols. in 8, Romae: Universitas Gregoriana, 1923-1938.

Woywod, Stanislaus, *A Practical Commentary on the Code of Canon Law,* 10. ed., 2 vols., New York: Wagner, 1946.

Zitelli, Zepherinus, *Apparatus Iuris Ecclesiastici,* Romae, 1886.

Articles

"A Pastor's Refusal of Baptism,"—*ER,* LXXXVII (1932), 524-526.

Anonymous, "Baptizing Children of Lapsed Parents," *The Clergy Review,* XXV (1945), 370.

———, "Blessing Baptismal Water in a Church without a Font," *ER, XCVI* (1937), 188.

———, "Is it lawful to baptize the Children of Catholics Who Implicitly Deny their Faith," *AER,* XX (1899), 297.

———, "Private Baptism," *ER,* LXXV (1926), 308-309.

———, "National Parishes: Affiliation and Separation,"—*ER,* LXXXVII (1932), 531.

———, "Notes on the Rubics of the Roman Ritual," n. 556; "Consecrating the Font at Pentecost in Rural Parishes," *ER,* LII (1915), 93.

Donovan, J. P., "What of This Baptismal Procedure in a State Hospital," *Homiletic and Pastoral Review,* XLIX (1948), 157.

Duffy, D. P., "Baptism in Cases of Difficult Parturition," *ER,* XLIX (1913), 613.

Oesterle, G., "De Baptismo Infantium e Tepidis Catholicis Progenitorum," *Jus Pontificium,* XVIII (1938), 186-191.

Waldron, J., "Hospital Baptisms," *The Jurist,* III (1943), 587-594.

Weber, Edward, "The Baptistery and Font," *The Homiletic and Pastoral Review,* XXVII (1927), 1288.

Woywod, S., "Baptism of Infants of Parents Whose Marriage is Invalid," *Homiletic and Pastoral Review,* XXIV (1924), 1063.

———, "Baptism in Private Houses," *Homiletic and Pastoral Review,* XXV (1924-25), 647.

———,"Blessing of Baptismal Water," *Homiletic and Pastoral Review,* XXIII (1923), 749.

———, "Concerning the Faculty to Baptize in a Private House outside the Case of Danger of Death," *Homiletic and Pastoral Review,* XXVI (1925-26), 299.

———, "Place of Baptistery," *Homiletic and Pastoral Review,* XXXVIII (1937-1938), 632.

———, "Recording of Baptism Conferred outside Proper Parish,"—*Homiletic and Pastoral Review,* XLI (1940-41), 87.

Periodicals

American Ecclesiastical Review, The (from July, 1905-December, 1943, *The Ecclesiastical Review*), Philadelphia, 1889-1943; Washington, D. C., 1944—.

Analecta Iuris Pontificii, Romae, 1855-1869; Parisiis, 1872-1891.

Clergy Review, The, London, 1931—.

Homiletic and Pastoral Review, The, New York, 1900—.

Jurist, The, Washington, D. C., 1941—.

Jus Pontificium, Romae, 1921-1940.

Monitore Ecclesiastico, Il, Maratea, 1876-1881; Conversano, 1882-1898; Roma, 1899-1948.

ABBREVIATIONS

AAS—*Acta Apostolicae Sedis.*
AER—*The American Ecclesiastical Review.*
ASS—*Acta Sanctae Sedis.*
Coll. Lac.—*Collectio Lacensis.*
CPI—*Collectio Pontificia Interpretationis.*
CV—*Corpus Scriptorum Ecclesiasticorum Latinorum.*
DTC—*Dictionnaire de Theologie Catholique.*
ER—*The Ecclesiastical Review.*
Fontes—*Codis Iuris Canonici Fontes cura . . . Gasparri editi.*
JK, JE,-JL—*Regesta Pontificum Romanorum etc.*
Mansi—*Sacrorum Conciliorum Nova et Amplissima Collectio.*
MGH—*Monumenta Germaniae Historica.*
MPG—Migne, *Patrologiae Graeca.*
MPL—Migne, *Patrologiae Latina.*
S. C. C.—Sacra Congregatio Concilii.
S. C. de Prop. Fide—Sacra Congregatio de Propaganda Fide.
S. C. de Sacramentis—Sacra Congregatio de Sacramentis.
S. C. S. Off.—Suprema Congregatio Sancti Officii.
S. R. C.—Sacrorum Rituum Congregatio.

BIOGRAPHICAL NOTE

Walter Joseph Conway was born on July 26, 1921, in Philadelphia, Pennsylvania. He attended St. Charles Borromeo Parochial School and Southeast Catholic High School of that city. In September of 1939 he was admitted into the Seminary of St. Charles Borromeo, Overbrook, Pennsylvania, where he received the degree of Bachelor of Arts in 1945. He was ordained to the sacred priesthood at Philadelphia on May 22, 1948. In the fall of that year he enrolled in the School of Canon Law of the Catholic University of America, where he received the degree of J.C.B. in June, 1949, and the degree of J.C.L. in June, 1950.

CANON LAW STUDIES*

322. Gaffigan, Rev. Aloysius J., O.S.F.S., J.C.L., Residence of Religious.
323. Cappiello, Rev. Linus V., O.F.M., J.C.L., De Ordinariorum Dispensandi Facultate ad Normam Canonis 81.
324. Conway, Rev. Walter J., J.C.L., The Time and Place of Baptism.
325. King, Rev. James P., J.C.L., The Canonical Procedure in Separation Cases.
326. Wrzaszczak, Rev. Chester F., J.C.L., The Betrothal Contract in the Code of Canon Law.

---

*A complete list of the previous numbers of this series will be found in the earlier studies. All the published numbers are available from the Catholic University of America Press, 620 Michigan Avenue, N.E., Washington 17, D. C., except the following: Nos. 1-116 inclusive, 118-123 inclusive, 128, 136, 144, 153, 162, 166, 175, 178, 182, 190 and 198. But the following numbers, now reissued, are obtainable from THE JURIST, The Catholic University of America, Washington 17, D. C., namely: Nos. 5, 7, 11, 17, 18, 19, 26, 28, 30, 34, 42, 44, 51, 52 and 61.

www.ingramcontent.com/pod-product-compliance
Lightning Source LLC
LaVergne TN
LVHW050224080826
844660LV00012B/467
* 9 7 8 0 8 1 3 2 2 4 9 5 4 *